# THE
# STENCILLING WORKBOOK

## COMPLETE STEP-BY-STEP DIRECTIONS
## AND PATTERNS FOR OVER 50 PROJECTS

## JUDY TUTTLE

A Garden Way Publishing Book

Storey Communications, Inc.
Schoolhouse Road
Pownal, Vermont 05261

Cover, interior design, and production by Carol Jessop
Edited by Gwen W. Steege
Illustrated by Carol Jessop
Cover and text photographs by Nicholas Whitman
Production assistance, Michelle Antonio

Printed in the United States by Courier
First printing, June 1991

# CONTENTS

# ACKNOWLEDGMENTS

One of the nicest things about stencilling is that once you try one project, you will find yourself thinking of dozens of other ways to use stencilling in the rooms you live in, on the clothes you wear, and for the gifts you give. The projects illustrated in 'A Color Scrapbook' (pages 89-96) were the result of that kind of creative energy, and many thanks are owed to Wanda Harper, Carol Jessop, Louise Lloyd, Pamela Mc Farland, and Lucy Sherrill, as well as to Novtex Factory Outlet in North Adams, MA, for contributing their enthusiasm and talents to produce the lively and varied objects displayed on those pages. We hope these examples will inspire your own efforts and that you will have as much fun stencilling as we did!

Gwen W. Steege
Editor

# INTRODUCTION

Whaat shall I do with that room? Paint? Wallpaper? If you had lived in the seventeenth-or eighteenth-century, you might have hired an itinerant artist to decorate your walls with stencilled borders, stencilled panels, and stencilled chair rails. He may have even stencilled your floor. You may have learned about him through a local newspaper (painters began advertising for work at the end of the eighteenth century) or you may have heard about him from your neighbor. Wandering artists tended to remain in a neighborhood as long as work was available; and several houses in one community might be decorated by one painter before he moved on.

The painter brought stencils cut from heavy paper and covered with many coats of oil, paint, or shellac to make them durable. He offered a limited choice of colors, perhaps a soft olive-green, an iron red, a dark blue, a black, or one of many shades of yellow. Ideas for patterns came from wallpapers (which were then extremely expensive) or from nature, drawn freehand by the artist. He often combined geometric shapes with leaves and flowers and topped the walls with swags and tassels in imitation of wallpaper borders. If you lived in colonial America, for example, your mostly wooden interior would be painted and then stencilled. In the nineteenth century, plastered walls were whitewashed or painted rose or buff before the stencil pattern was applied.

Stencilling is still a most creative and interesting way to decorate. Patterns may be chosen to bring color to old homes under restoration, as well as to enhance the most contemporary decor. Designs drawn from nature and geometry are appropriate for country homes, while ornate, formal patterns look best in the high-ceilinged rooms of Victorian houses, embellished with elaborate moldings and woodwork; modern interiors can sport bands of bright colors that stand in stark contrast to the simple lines of the architecture. Design combinations can be varied to suit anyone's taste and can be made to complement existing furnishings and color schemes. Stencilled surfaces can easily be scrubbed when soil or stains appear. In short, with stencils anyone can create a handsome, unique, and personalized interior.

Stencilling may be used not only to decorate walls and floors, but also to adorn drapes, quilts, rugs, lampshades, furniture, and even such incidentals as napkin rings and stationery. Guest towels can be stencilled and embroidered; baby bibs and tee shirts can be decorated as gifts for the newborn. Beautiful, one-of-a-kind gift wrap can be created by stencilling on white or green freezer paper, while stencilled throw pillows, tote bags, and sweatshirts make ideal presents.

As distinctive as stencilling is, it is also inexpensive, little practice is needed to become proficient at it, and it takes surprisingly little time to complete a project. Children can learn to stencil and turn out enviable results with paint or even crayons. Organizations can use stencilling on items they sell, and businesses often display stencilled logos. Stencilled designs can be neatly applied, with minimum mess, and mistakes can be easily corrected. No expensive equipment or special talent is necessary — all it takes is the desire to create something unique and have fun doing it.

# 1 STENCILLING BASICS

The concept of stencilling is uncomplicated: One applies color through a hole cut in a piece of stencil material, which is held against the surface being decorated. The cut-out image may be printed over and over again — as long as the stencil material holds up. One of the few limitations on the design is that, in order to keep the stencil stable, large areas must be broken into smaller segments separated by "bridges." The way in which a design is segmented gives it its distinctively stencilled look.

The materials needed for stencilling are also simple: a flat sheet from which to cut the design, a cutting tool, color, and a color applicator. In this chapter, you will find suggested materials and their advantages and disadvantages, as well as information about how to design and apply stencils.

## EQUIPMENT AND MATERIALS

### CUTTING TOOLS

To cut a stencil accurately, you will need either an instrument with a very sharp blade or an electric stencil cutting pen. A *craft*, or *X-acto knife*, cuts both curved and straight lines well; and because it is pencil sized, it is easy to manipulate. Use a straight-edged, pointed blade; X-acto makes one blade (No. 16) specifically for stencilling. If you need a very heavy stencil (leather or heavy cardboard, for example), you may wish to use a *utility knife*. Its large handle should be gripped tightly in the palm of your hand. Straight lines are easy to cut with a utility knife, but curved ones are more difficult. Both of these tools are extremely sharp, so take care not to cut yourself and keep them out of reach of children when you aren't working. Also, protect your work surface with a thick layer of newspaper or an old magazine.

Very simple stencils may be cut with *scissors*. Thin scissors (manicure or embroidery scissors, for example) are best, as it is fairly easy to thrust the point through the paper to begin the cut. Scissors are a little more difficult to manipulate around right-angle cuts. With patience, however, even very intricate designs may be cut with sharp scissors that are small enough to use for complicated designs.

Mylar stencils (see page 2) may also be cut quickly, easily, and accurately with a *stencil cutting pen*, available at art supply and craft stores that sell stencilling materi-

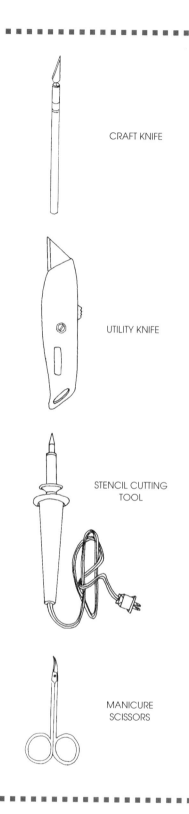

CRAFT KNIFE

UTILITY KNIFE

STENCIL CUTTING
TOOL

MANICURE
SCISSORS

als. This tool resembles a wood-burning pen, and requires the same safety precautions — do not touch the hot metal, do not allow the hot tip to rest on a flammable surface, unplug the tool after use, and *always supervise its use by children (young children should not use it at all)*. To use a stencil cutting pen, place the pattern you are tracing on a hard, smooth surface and tape a sheet of Mylar securely to the pattern. Grip the pen as you would a pencil and draw the tip along the line to be cut. The pen works best when moved toward you, so you will have to move the pattern and stencil as you work; lift the pen when you turn the stencil. Keep the pen as upright as possible, so that the fine point, rather than the broad side does the "cutting." You will need to apply only light pressure; move the pen at a moderate speed. If residue builds on the tip, remove it by rubbing the tip gently with fine steel wool.

Whatever cutting tool you use, cut some practice stencils before attempting a finished product. You may feel awkward at first, and a few slips or ruined cutouts are inevitable. Before long, you will find you can cut even intricate patterns with ease.

## THE STENCIL ITSELF

*Heavy, oiled stencil paper*, which can be bought in many art stores, has long been used for stencilling. It is fairly easy to cut with an X-acto knife, the oil on it keeps it from becoming soggy with paint, and it is easily cleaned. It is thin enough so that you can get sharp, exact pattern lines, and sturdy enough so

the scrubbing motion of stencil brushes doesn't tear it. You can make your own oiled stencil sheets by coating manila oak tag (such as a file folder) with a 50-50 mixture of boiled linseed oil and turpentine; hang the sheets until they are dry. The main disadvantages of these stencil sheets are that they are opaque and they warp after heavy use.

A good alternative to oiled stencil paper is a polyester film sold under the brand name *Mylar*. It is available in 9" x 12" (23 cm x 30 cm) and 12" x 18" (30 cm x 45 cm) sheets, as well as rolls. Because Mylar is transparent, it is convenient for both tracing designs and aligning the stencil while you are printing. It is more flexible than oiled paper, however, and some people thus find it a little harder to handle when stencilling long horizontal patterns on walls. If you use a knife, Mylar is also a little more difficult for the beginner to cut than is oiled paper; a stencil cutting pen, however, makes Mylar easy to cut.

*Other good-quality papers* may be used if sprayed with several coats of polyurethane (allow to dry thoroughly between coats). The polyurethane stiffens the paper and keeps it from disintegrating when paint is applied. Papers treated this way don't hold up as well during clean-up as oiled stencil paper or Mylar stencils, and their opacity makes it difficult or impossible to trace the stencil design.

Some art stores and museum gift shops sell *ready-made brass stencils*. These work very well on flat surfaces, but they are not flexible enough to bend around corners. They are easy to clean, however, may be held with one hand while stencilling, and last indefinitely.

## BRUSHES AND OTHER PAINT APPLICATORS

*Stencil brushes* come in a wide variety of sizes; the nature and size of the project will dictate the size brush you need. For stencilling large areas, large brushes (1 inch) (2.5 cm) give better, more even coverage. For narrow, dainty borders or designs with small figures, a brush ½ inch (1.2 cm) or smaller works best. Stencil brushes have blunt-cut bristles. You may find some have softer bristles than others; experiment to discover which gives the best texture for the project you are planning. You will need a stiffer brush for stencilling on fabric than for printing on paper.

For some projects, instead of brushes, you may wish to use *sponges* to achieve interesting textural effects. Cut new, inexpensive sponges (they will be soft when first removed from the package) to the desired size, and either blot or scrub the paint through the stencil opening.

*Trim rollers* with short-napped covers are available at any paint store and can be used to apply color more quickly than either brushes or sponges. They become sticky, however, if used with anything other than an oil-based paint.

Be sure to clean your brushes thoroughly before drying and storing them. Rinse them in the solvent needed for your paint (water for acrylics, mineral spirits for oils),

and then wash them carefully in warm (never hot), soapy water. Allow them to dry completely before storing them. If you wish to interrupt your stencilling for short periods, you can wrap your brushes with plastic cling film and refrigerate them to keep them moist.

## OTHER SUPPLIES YOU MAY NEED

Because stencil paint is applied very, very sparsely (a few tablespoons will be enough for most ceiling borders, for instance), you will need a *piece of glass, a paint tray, or some other nonabsorbent surface* on which to pour a few drops of your paint. If you were to dip the brush into the paint jar and try to print immediately, you would get too much paint on the brush. You will also need *a piece of scrap paper* (paper towel works well) on which to rub excess paint from the brush. If you plan to mix colors you will need *several small containers*.

It is important to use *a measuring tool*, such as a yardstick or tape measure, to determine placement of the design on the item to be stencilled, be it wall, drapery fabric, paper, furniture, or cloth. For marking very large spaces, such as a floor, you may need *a chalk line* (available in hardware stores), to help keep lines straight. A *level* is useful for creating an exactly horizontal or vertical line on a wall that is not quite square.

*Adhesive stencil spray* is popular with many stencillers, especially when using large, floppy stencils or when stencilling on curved or slippery surfaces. Protect the surrounding area from excess spray,

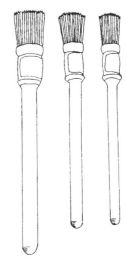

STENCIL BRUSHES

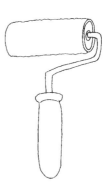

TRIM ROLLER

SPONGE

use proper ventilation, and spray only lightly. If you are stencilling on a painted surface, be sure it is completely dry, or the adhesive may pull up the paint.

If stripes are to be a part of the stencil design, *a roll of 3-inch (7.5 cm) wide masking tape or painter's tape* (a kraft paper designed for this purpose), half gummed and half plain, is helpful. This tape is available at hardware and paint stores. The technique for using tape to screen off areas for painting is the same no matter how wide the stripe. Tape is laid along the guide lines described in project instructions. The gummed edge of the tape is placed on the line and the ungummed edge of the tape is away from the stripe. A second strip of tape is laid along the other side of the stripe. It is important to measure the spacing between the two strips of tape frequently and carefully; wavering or uneven stripes will be obvious to the eye when the tape is removed. Depending on the surface being printed, paint may be applied between the two strips of tape with a trim roller or a brush. (See illustration at left.)

Also important to have on hand are *paint sticks* for stirring; *paint thinner or water* for cleaning stencils and tools (use whatever solvent is recommended by the paint manufacturer); *clean rags* for wiping off mistakes; and *small artists' brushes* for touch-ups.

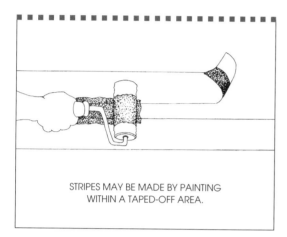
STRIPES MAY BE MADE BY PAINTING WITHIN A TAPED-OFF AREA.

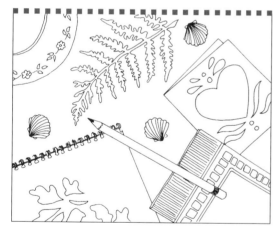
DESIGN IDEAS ARE ALL AROUND YOU.

## CREATING THE DESIGN

"What should I use for a design?" is often the first question that comes to mind when one is faced with a stencilling project. The design, its size, and the colors used are all contingent upon where the stencilling is to be applied. Foot-tall (30 cm) stencils make elegant ceiling borders in a high-ceilinged room; inch-high (2.5 cm) stencils are just right for a pillowcase border. Three-inch (7.5 cm) borders fit nicely around most door and window frames; ¾-inch (1.9 cm) ducks look fine on baby's bib and tee shirt.

It is easier to design your own stencil pattern than you may think. Geometric patterns, designs taken from nature, or traditional figures may be traced or drawn freehand. For leaves, fruit, and flowers, for instance, simply trace around plant materials found in your yard and garden or along the street. Take ideas from lace, wallpaper books, tablecloths, and china. Use traditional stencil patterns, such as hearts, houses, swags, tassels, and teapots. Think of a favorite theme — nautical designs, for example, include sailboats and anchors. Look in children's books for such figures as animals; coloring books, in particular, may offer dozens of simple shapes, ready to trace. Sit down with a piece of graph paper and develop geometric designs by coloring in the squares, then rounding the edges. Don't be afraid to experiment. Keep in mind, however, a basic principle of stencilling: long lines need to be broken every 3 inches (7.5 cm) or so with a "bridge" to reinforce the stencil.

Your personal taste, of course, will determine what colors you use. You may choose the stencil colors for a ceiling border according to the woodwork colors in the room, or vice versa. A picture, a rug, the colors in the upholstery or drapes all can suggest colors for wall stencils. Usually the simpler the color scheme, the more attractive is the stencil design. One or two colors almost always look elegant on walls, floors, and even on cloth. Before cutting the stencil, decide how many colors you would like to use and in what manner, because usually it is best to cut a separate stencil for each color.

## CUTTING SINGLE-COLOR STENCILS

Begin by tracing or photocopying your design. If the stencil material is transparent, place it over the copy, and tape the stencil in place to insure that it does not move while you are cutting. (See illustration at right.) Be sure to center the design on the stencil, with at least a 2-inch (5 cm) border all around, so that you will have room for your brush when you print and not have to worry about getting paint where it isn't wanted. Position your designs on the stencils so that they are centered and parallel to the edges, when possible. Many times you can use the edge of the stencil as a guide for placing the design. (If your stencil material is

opaque, you will have to use carbon paper to mark the design on the stencil before cutting.)

To cut the stencil, place it on a smooth surface, protected by a thick layer of paper. Holding the knife as you would hold a pencil, cut along the lines of the design. (See pages 1-2 for use of an electric stencil cutting pen.) Most people find it easiest to cut toward themselves by moving the stencil as necessary while cutting. When you have cut completely around a shape, lift out the material you cut away, to form the spaces through which the paint will be applied. All parts of a single-colored design may be cut from one stencil sheet.

## CUTTING MULTI-COLORED STENCILS

If your design consists of more than one color, it is usually best to cut one stencil for each color. For the first color, place the stencil paper over the design and trace only the parts of the design that are to be in that color. Center the design on the stencil paper, leaving at least a 2-inch (5 cm) border all around the design. Cut out the first stencil.

Place a second stencil sheet over the original design (again leaving a 2-inch (5 cm) border), and trace and cut out the parts of the design

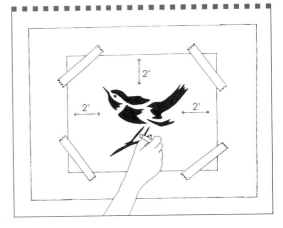

TAPE THE STENCIL MATERIAL TO THE PATTERN AND LEAVE A 2-INCH BORDER AROUND THE DESIGN.

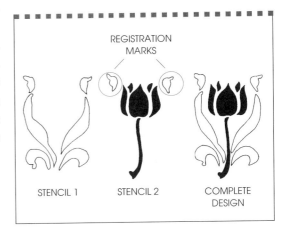

CUTTING AND REGISTERING TWO-COLOR STENCILS

that are to be in the second color. To position the second color accurately, you must make guides called *registration marks* on this stencil. These can be two small dots on either side of the design (usually on the center line) or portions of the first design. If you use dots, cut them in both stencils; when you print the first stencil, make light pencil dots through the registration marks that you can use to align the second stencil. If you use transparent stencil material (such as Mylar), you may prefer to trace portions of the first design onto the second to use for positioning. (See illustration on page 5.) After both stencils are cut, make a sample print so that you can ascertain that your registration marks have been accurately placed.

If the design consists of three or more colors, follow the same technique for additional stencils, one for each color. Be sure to leave a 2-inch (5 cm) border on each stencil and to cut or draw registration marks on each.

## PLANNING COLORS AND CHOOSING PAINT

A wide variety of colors and many kinds of paint may be used for stencilling. Some projects may require a very particular color, and you may wish to mix your own paint. If you do, be sure that you use the same kinds of paints — oil-based with oil-based, japan paints with japan paints, acrylic with acrylic. Red, yellow, and blue are the primary colors from which other colors can be mixed. Green, orange, and purple can be easily

made from the primary colors; browns and blacks will darken any of the colors. It is very important to mix enough of the desired color to complete the stencil project — it is extremely difficult to duplicate a hand-mixed shade. Also, proceed slowly: only a small amount of added color can radically change some hues.

## ADVANTAGES OF THE VARIOUS KINDS OF PAINTS

Many shades of japan paints are available in art stores. These oil-based paints dry quickly to a flat finish, are easily mixed, and can be manipulated to provide beautiful shading. If you desire a slightly more glossy finish, use a satin-finish, oil-based enamel, such as you would use for interior trim. Use good-quality, thick paint that won't run when it is applied. Follow directions on the paint can for paint removal if you must remove paint that gets where you don't want it.

*Acrylic paint*, which is water-based, has the advantage of being easy to remove if a mistake is made, but it dries very quickly on the stencil and may make some stencils curl or become unstable. If you use acrylics, the stencils tend to get sticky and you may have to clean them more often than if you use oil-based paints. Acrylics have the advantage, however, of being more opaque than some of the other stencil paints.

For stencilling on fabric, a *textile screen-printing ink* gives beautiful results. Available at art stores in a wide variety of colors, these paints mix easily and are thick enough to work well through stencils. Fabric and craft stores also sell *fabric dyes* and *fabric paints* formulated for use on cloth. These sometimes require the addition of a medium, which thins the paint, making it easier to work with and more readily absorbed by the fabric. Follow the manufacturer's instructions for use. Whatever you choose, you will probably have to set the colors with heat, so that the design doesn't launder out. Again, follow the manufacturer's instructions carefully. Before heat setting, however, colors may often be washed out — a great convenience if a mistake is made. For more information about fabric paints, see pages 103-104.

*Spray paint* may be applied through stencils. Spray is difficult to control, however, and you must provide a very wide border on the stencil to avoid getting color outside the design. You must also take care not to spray the paint on so thickly that it runs; many very light coats work better than one heavy one.

Even *crayons, pastels, and marking pens* may be used with stencils. Care must be taken with these media to apply colors lightly so that you don't get a darker-colored ridge around the outside of the stencil pattern. Some are also difficult to clean away if mistakes are made.

For information about stencilling with *metallic powders*, see pages 85-86.

### SHADING STENCILLED SHAPES

In the eighteenth century, the paint in stencil designs was usually applied lightly, with the tone flat and even throughout. You may prefer, however, to create a different effect by shading the color in each shape. This is accomplished by applying the paint around the edges of the stencil and letting it fade subtly to little or no paint in the center. This is especially effective when you are stencilling round objects, such as fruits or vases. (See color pages 90 and 91). You may also add decorative accents by applying a second coat of the same color as the dried base coat, in order, for example, to make a darker crest on the head of a bird. Or, add a second color to get a more realistic effect — for instance, brush a slight bit of orange onto the lower part of a yellow pear.

## PLACING THE DESIGN

Before deciding exactly where to place the design, consider the existing lines of the object or space on which you are stencilling. On a pillowcase, for instance, the border stitching provides a straight guide line; the edge of a greeting card serves the same purpose.

Straight lines, however, don't necessarily exist when you are working on a ceiling, which can slope down at one side or arch in the middle. Before applying a stencilled border along a ceiling, place a level in several spots along the wall where it meets the ceiling. Very small variations off level won't be noticeable, and you can simply let the border follow the ceiling line. If the ceiling is very uneven, however, you will have to use the level as a guide to draw a straight

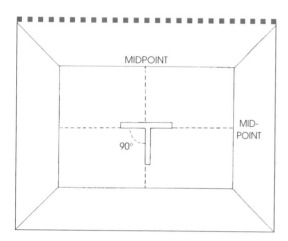

MIDPOINT

MID-POINT

90°

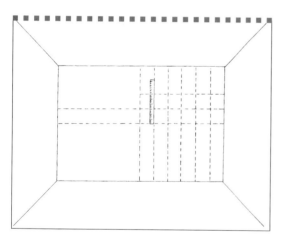

HOW TO MAKE A GRID FOR DESIGN PLACEMENT: *(ABOVE)* USE A T SQUARE TO FIND THE CENTER RIGHT-ANGLE INTERSECTION; *(BELOW)* MEASURE AND MARK THE GRID.

line. If the ceilings in your house are crooked, chances are that the corners aren't square either, and to get true verticals you will again have to use a level as a guide. For further information, see page 14.

Large, flat areas — whether on a wall, a floor, or a quilt — may need to be divided into grids to help you space the design evenly. Measure the width of the space at both top and bottom; divide each width by two, and mark the halfway points. Measure the length along both sides, and mark the halfway points. If you connect both pairs of marks, the point where the two lines intersect is the center. If your space is not exactly square or rectangular, however, the lines won't intersect at right angles to each other. If you construct a grid with those lines as references, the squares you measure will become more and more uneven as you get toward the edges of the space; a mistake of ¼ inch (6 mm) in the center can become a 2-inch (5 cm) mistake at the outside. To correct this problem, place a square or T square along the lines and assess whether the angles are exactly square at their intersections; adjust accordingly. (See illustration at left.)

Once you have intersecting center lines at right angles to each other, construct a grid by measuring out the desired distance from each of the center lines. When finished, the flat surface will resemble a checkerboard on which you can easily locate your patterns. (See illustration at left.)

## APPLYING PAINT

The most common mistake for beginners is to apply too much paint. The result is smeared and dripping paint, soggy stencils, and discouraged artists. Remember, a couple of tablespoons of paint is enough to stencil a border for an entire room, so very little is needed for each print.

Begin by positioning your stencil where you wish to print, and tape it in place. Next, stir or shake the paint, if necessary, and dribble a small amount on a paint tray or a piece of glass or plastic. Scrub the stencil brush in a circular motion until some paint has been taken up. On a piece of scrap paper, scrub this little bit of paint out of the brush until only a faint shade shows. For best results, stencilling must be done with a very dry brush. Holding the brush upright, apply the paint through the stencil in a circular, scrubbing motion, as though you were a child scribbling on a piece of paper. (See illustrations on page 9.) It is usually best to work from the edge of the stencil toward the center of the area being printed. When you have scrubbed over all of the open areas of your design, remove the stencil and observe how much paint has been applied. Before printing the next stencil, you may need to add more paint to the brush. Again, don't take up too much, and wipe the brush on scrap paper before applying your design. If your print smears or runs in any way, you have probably used too much paint.

When it is time to change colors, clean your brush well and allow it to dry completely before attempting to print with the next color. Wet brushes are likely to result in blurred or different colored prints. In order to save time, you may wish to have a collection of brushes on hand.

When you apply paint with a roller, the technique is similar. Dribble a small amount of paint on a paint tray or glass in an S motion. Roll a short-napped roller over the paint until it just coats the roller surface. Remove most of the paint by rolling it onto a piece of scrap paper, and then apply the remaining paint through the stencil.

A sponge should also be nearly dry before a good stencil print can be made. Pick up a little paint on the sponge and blot it almost dry on a piece of scrap paper. Blot or scrub over the open areas on the stencil.

It is best to practice in an area where it won't show, like the back of a closet or in the garage. You will be surprised at how quickly you become expert. After applying two or three prints to the garage wall, or even to a piece of newsprint taped to a wall or table, you will be ready to begin your project.

## DEALING WITH PROBLEMS

### CORRECTING MISTAKES

On surfaces other than fabric, you can usually clean up mistakes with a clean cloth saturated with the solvent required to thin your paint. If you are using oil-based paint, for example, use turpentine or other paint thinner to remove the print. Prints made with water-based paints may be cleaned up with soap and water on a clean cloth. Once the mistake has been removed, allow plenty of time — at least an hour — for the surface to dry before trying to print again, or the print will smear or take on a different color or texture from the rest of the project. If the removal of the design has somehow changed the background color or texture, with a clean cloth or small artist brush repaint the background and allow it to dry completely before reapplying the print.

If the project is complete and dry before the mistake is discovered, sand lightly to remove the error, and reapply enough coats of background color to cover the area completely. Print the stencil again.

Mistakes on cloth can usually be washed out with detergent and water, as long as you haven't yet ironed the piece to set the color. Repeated washings may be necessary to get out all the color, and

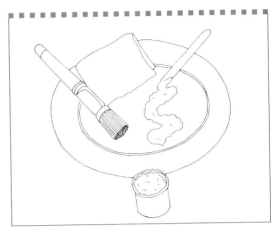

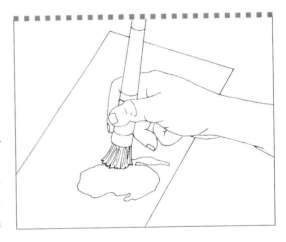

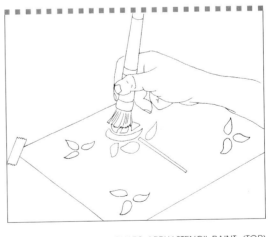

HOW TO APPLY STENCIL PAINT: *(TOP)* DRIBBLE A SMALL AMOUNT OF PAINT ON A PALETTE; *(MIDDLE)* BLOT EXCESS PAINT FROM BRUSH ONTO SCRAP PAPER; *(BOTTOM)* SCRUB OR DAB PAINT THROUGH STENCIL OPENINGS.

some fabrics and/or paints may never clean completely. Good designs, too, are usually taken out with the mistakes.

No matter what the project, it is best not to try to repaint over a print once it is on the project, for it is nearly impossible to position the stencil exactly where it was in the first place and you will in all likelihood get a blurred print. If part of a design is removed because of an error, you should repaint only that part of the design.

### ROUGH SURFACES

Many times — on walls of old houses, for instance — the surface to be stencilled is rough. When paint is applied to a rough surface, dark lines of paint will appear on raised irregularities. To avoid these lines, it is particularly important to stencil with a very dry brush. Pick up paint with the brush, and rub it off on your scrap paper even more completely than usual — until you see almost *no* color coming off. Tape your stencil in place, and scrub in your design lightly. Leave the stencil taped down, allow the print to dry thoroughly, and repeat the process. Continue applications until the color is the desired intensity.

### HARD-TO-REACH PLACES

For hard-to-reach places (such as behind a radiator), you may find it necessary to use something other than a brush to apply the paint. If there is enough room, tape the stencil in place, and use a small trim roller; be sure it is as dry as the brush you've been using. Instead

of a roller, you may find it easier to manipulate a small piece of sponge. Cover the sponge with paint, blot it on scrap paper until very little color comes off, and then hold the sponge between your first and second fingers so that you can slide your hand into the narrow space and apply the paint.

Some spots are so difficult that no tool will fit well enough to apply paint. The beauty of stencilling, as opposed to wallpaper, is that the difficult spot may be skipped altogether without detracting from the overall appearance of the stencilling project. Blank spaces are hardly noticeable as long as the background color is consistent throughout.

## CLEANING THE STENCIL

Even when you use a very dry brush, you may occasionally get a spot of paint on the back of the stencil — and this spot will most certainly rub off on the wall, spoiling your next print. To avoid this, check the back of the stencil after each print. When necessary, put it face down on a piece of newspaper or paper towel and gently wipe the back with a soft cloth or tissue. After ten or twelve prints, the stencil will begin to get sticky. If it moves even a fraction of an inch at this point, the edges will blur. The stencil must therefore be cleaned. When you use very thick paint or acrylic paint, you may have to clean your stencils more frequently. Place the stencil, right side up, on two or three sheets of newspaper spread on top of one another. Pour a very small amount of paint thinner or water (whatever medium you use to thin your paint) over the stencil, and with a very clean cloth, gently rub the paint off the stencil. When it is free of paint, turn it over and place it on fresh newspaper to clean the other side. Remember that stencils — especially the narrow bridges — can tear, so don't be too vigorous in the cleaning process. Allow the stencil to dry, or dry it with another clean cloth before making any more prints.

When you are finished with your stencils, clean them thoroughly as described above, allow them to dry completely, and store them flat.

# HOW TO USE THE PATTERNS IN THIS BOOK

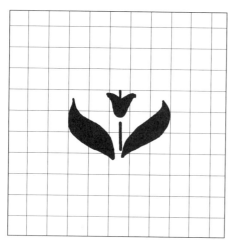

1 SQUARE = 1 INCH

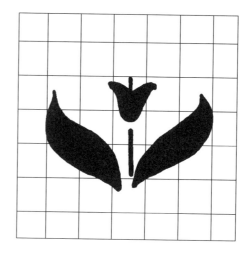

1 SQUARE = 2 INCHES

## 1

The patterns that are overlaid with a grid (1 square=1 inch (2.5 cm) ) will need to be enlarged. To make the enlargement, on a blank sheet of paper make a 1-inch (2.5 cm) grid and copy the pattern square by square. In some cases, depending on the scale of the room or object on which you are stencilling, you may wish to enlarge the design even more (or perhaps even to reduce it). The easiest way to do this is to use the enlargement/reduction feature on a photocopier. If you don't have access to such a machine, you can again use the grid on the pattern. Calculate the size to which you want to enlarge or reduce the pattern, and make your blank grid whatever size is needed to produce the proper scale. Please note that because projects differ, each materials list can only estimate quantities of supplies.

## 2

Color is a very personal matter, and for home decorating stencils in particular, the colors you choose will be determined by your own taste and your color schemes. For this reason, the book does not indicate particular colors for most of the designs. Instead, patterns are shown in two or more shades, so that you can see which parts of a design might be printed in the same colors. You may prefer other combinations or even an entire design stencilled in only one color. (See pages 5-6 for more on the use of color.)

You will usually find it convenient to print all of the stencils of a particular color at one time. Clean your brush and allow it to dry *completely* before using it for another color. If you try to use a damp brush, the color will not be true and the print is likely to run or blur.

## 3

Registration marks are indicated by the symbol ⊕ ; some patterns show center marks (**X**) instead of or as well as registration marks. Be sure to cut or mark these on your stencils as guides to position prints accurately. Repeats are indicated by a broken line.

# 2 STENCILLING WALLS

Perfect walls are not a prerequisite for decorative stencilling; in fact, on fairly rough walls you can replicate antique effects quite nicely. Wallpaper should be removed before you paint the walls. Although it is often very difficult to remove wallpaper that has been painted over, it is worth the effort to provide a good background for your hand-painted stencilling. Although stencilling can be done on painted-over wallpaper, of course, the wallpaper seams will show through the background paint, and the prints that occur over a seam may pick up a dark line.

If the walls have holes or large cracks, fill them with spackling compound (available at hardware and paint stores). Scrape off any loose paint with a steel-bristled brush or sandpaper, and smooth the rough edges with spackling. When the spackling has dried, smooth the surface with fairly fine sandpaper, and prime the area with a paint undercoater. Make sure the entire wall is clean, or your paint won't adhere well.

A background of very light colored flat paint provides the most antique effect for stencil patterns. White and off-white are always successful, but a very light green or faintly rose-tinged shade make a stunning room also. If you are striving for a contemporary appearance, it is particularly important to prepare a smooth, clean surface. Sand rough places, and patch cracks. The background paint can be of any color, but a flat, rather than a glossy, paint takes a stencil print best.

## BORDERS

Many rooms have no wall decoration other than stencilled borders. This makes it possible to arrange pictures and other wall hangings without competition. Borders can be of any width from 3 to 12 inches (7.5 to 30 cm); they can be composed of anything from a large, geometric design to a small vine and flower. The usual rule is for the height of the ceiling to dictate the size of the stencil — higher ceilings require larger patterns. For instance, an average room with a 7½-foot (2.3 m) ceiling looks nice with a 6-inch (15 cm) border, but if window casings reach within 6 inches (15 cm) of the ceiling, a smaller design may be necessary, so that the complete design will flow in a continuous line all the way around the room.

If you have trouble visualizing how large a stencil you should use, simulate a border by drawing your design on paper (use marking pens or shapes cut from colored construction paper to approximate the colors) and taping it to the wall where you plan to stencil. When you stand back from it you should be able to judge whether the final design should be larger or smaller.

You need not clear out a room or even cover things when you stencil a border; the paint is so dry when it is applied that there are no drips or runs. It is easier to work on a ceiling border, however, if curtains are out of the way.

USE A LEVEL TO MARK TRUE VERTICALS AND HORIZONTALS.

To determine if the ceiling line is straight, hold a level along the top of the wall where the ceiling meets it in several places. If the variations are small, you can simply follow the ceiling line. If the top of the wall is very irregular, however, you will have to create a straight, true horizontal line. At the place where the ceiling is lowest, hold the level exactly even so that the bubble is centered. Draw a very light, straight line using the level as a guide. Slide the level over so that a foot of it still runs along the line you have just drawn. Again, check the bubble, and continue drawing the line. Proceed all the way around the room in this manner. (See illustration at left.)

## STENCILLING INDIVIDUAL PATTERNS AS A BORDER

Ceiling borders may be made up of individual designs placed next to each other, or of a running design, such as a vine that forms a continuous pattern around the room.

If you are stencilling a continuous line of *individual* stencil patterns, plan the spacing so no design will run into the corner, if possible. To do this, measure the design unit, and add the number of inches needed between it and the next design. For example, if the stencil pattern takes up 5 inches (13 cm), and you want 1 inch (2.5 cm) between patterns, a complete design equals 6 inches (15 cm). Measure the space to be stencilled, edge to edge, and divide this measurement by 6 inches (15 cm) to find the number of repeats to be stencilled. If the number doesn't come out even, part of a design (or a part of a space) will fall into the corner. To correct this, make the amount of space between designs longer or shorter until there is room for either a whole design or a whole space at each end. (See illustrations at right.)

If the border design is to go all the way around a room without interruption, measure the whole way around the room and divide that number of inches by the number of inches required for a complete design (the design plus the space between designs). For a 4-inch (10 cm) design spaced 4 inches (10 cm) apart, divide the total number of inches around the room by 8 inches (20 cm). For example, for a 12-foot (3.6 m) by 12-foot (3.6 m) room you would divide 576 inches (1440 cm) by 8 inches (20 cm) to determine that the room will have 72 designs spaced 4 inches (10 cm) apart. Make adjustments as necessary, so that when the final design is applied, it will be spaced perfectly next to the very first design. Because it is usually better not to have an individual design "turn the corner," you may wish to measure each border on a wall-by-wall basis, even when the pattern continues all the way around the room.

### STENCILLING A RUNNING DESIGN AS A BORDER

If you are stencilling a continuous border, without a beginning or end, choose the least conspicuous place to start in — the corner of a room or a doorway, for instance. The beginning and end of stencils that make a long border rarely match

up exactly where they meet. When you reach a corner, bend the stencil to fit and tape it in place; this will leave both your hands free to apply the paint properly. For the first design, place the edge of the stencil along the line planned for it, apply the paint, and lift the stencil. Move the stencil to the right and match the first holes of the stencil to the last holes painted (these are indicated by a broken line on the pattern). Do not repaint the print you match. (See illustration on page 16.) Continue in this manner until the last design is about to run into the first applied. It is unlikely that there will be an exact match, so stencil up to where the paint from the first print shows through, and stop. (The techniques for planning and applying individual patterns and continuous running designs for borders are the same for furniture and fabric projects as for walls.)

### CHAIR RAILS AND OTHER ARCHITECTURAL FEATURES

Some old houses have chair rails, which can be enhanced by a stencilled border. Even if a room doesn't have one, you can run a stencil design about 36 to 40 inches (90 to 102 cm) from the floor and create the effect of one — an interesting design feature in both modern and older homes. Use a

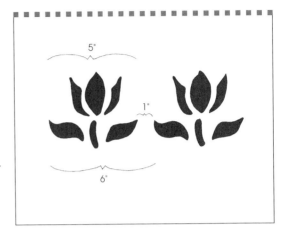

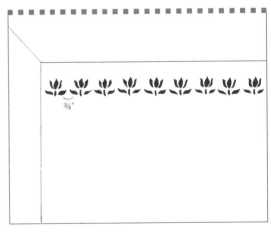

HOW TO PLAN INDIVIDUAL PATTERNS IN A BORDER: (ABOVE) MEASURE THE WIDTH OF EACH DESIGN, INCLUDING THE PATTERN AND THE SPACE BETWEEN PATTERNS; (BELOW) ADJUST SPACING BETWEEN PATTERNS, IF NECESSARY, SO THAT THERE IS ROOM FOR A WHOLE DESIGN AT EACH END OF THE BORDER.

level to create a line at the appropriate height. A 3- to 4-inch high (7.5 to 10 cm) stencil border consisting of either a running design or individual patterns placed very close together would be appropriate. The area above the "chair rail" can be stencilled with an overall design, with or without a ceiling border, or a ceiling border alone can be applied. Use a single color or several, coordinated with the color scheme of the room.

You may wish to stencil part or all of the ceiling border along the baseboard, and/or around door frames and window frames. It is common for the baseboard pattern to be smaller in width than the ceiling border, but of similar colors and with motifs repeated from the ceiling design. In colonial homes, however, many different patterns were often used in one room with fine effect, so don't feel confined to one pattern per room.

## PROTECTING YOUR WORK

Stencilling done with oil paint on a clean, flat background will last for a very long time — even centuries. Wait a full week for the stencil paint to set completely, then wash off pencil and chalk marks. Thereafter, the walls can be washed as needed. If a stencilled wall is to be subjected to very heavy wear (such as in a stairwell), cover it with a coat of clear finish. To make sure that the protective coat is compatible with the stencil paint you have used, ask at your paint or hardware store. There isn't usually any problem if you have used flat or satin-finish paints, but after so much effort you don't want to take chances. Check, too, to be sure that what you apply for extra protection won't yellow after a few years and spoil your work. On a white or off-white wall, especially, don't use a product unless you have a guarantee that it won't yellow.

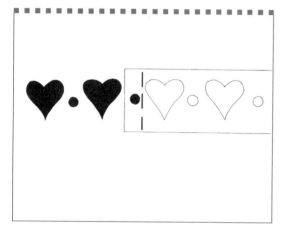

FOR CONTINUOUS BORDERS, MATCH THE LEFT OPENING ON THE STENCIL WITH THE LAST PART OF THE PRINTED DESIGN; DO NOT PAINT OVER PRINTED PORTION.

*(color page 96)*

Because hall furniture is often limited to a very few pieces, it is one place where stencilling really stands out. A chair rail and small motifs for each stair tread are features of this project.

## MATERIALS

Flat wall paint

Six 12" x 18" (30 cm x 45 cm) stencil sheets and cutting tool

Tape measure and level

Stencil paints (2 colors)

Stencil brush

Paint tray

Scrap paper

Paint thinner and clean cloths

**1**

Prepare the walls and paint the hall the background color you have chosen. Flat paint takes a stencil best.

**2**

If your floors are level, measure up 36 inches (90 cm) from the floor all around both upper and lower halls, and draw a guide line for the chair rail. (If your floors are not even, place a level along your 36-inch-high (90 cm) marks. Adjust as necessary and use the level as a guide to make the line.) To determine the height of the chair rail along the stairs, measure the height of the stair railing and mark a line for your stencilled chair rail at the same height.

**3**

Measure down 5 inches (13 cm) from the ceiling both downstairs and upstairs for the ceiling border. Use the level to determine whether adjustments are needed before drawing the guide line. If the ceiling is level, you can use the edge of your stencil to keep you on a straight line along the ceiling.

**4**

Start stencilling the chair rail at some natural breaking point, such as a door. Place the stencil for the broken line so that the top of the design (*not* the edge of the stencil) just touches the line made at 36 inches (90 cm). Stencil the design according to the instructions for printing continuous borders on pages 15-16. Continue the border up the stairs, following the line you made. When you come to a door or window, simply break the design and pick up again on the other side.

**5**

Print the circular motif within the broken lines in another color; use the registration marks for positioning.

**6**

Stencil the broken line and flowers for the ceiling border. Place the broken line on the guide line drawn in Step 3, and use the same color you used for the broken line of the chair rail in Step 4. The most difficult part will be reaching the portion of the wall over the stairwell. Because the configuration of every hallway is different, there is no one technique that will suggest how best to accomplish this task. If you have to rig a temporary scaffolding, you may be able to prop a ladder against the wall opposite the stair landing and then place heavy boards (2" x 8" or 2" x 10") (5 cm x 20 cm or 5 cm x 25 cm) level from the landing across to a ladder rung to form a platform. Be sure to make your scaffolding as safe as possible: Planking should be sturdy and wide, and ladders should be seated securely, so that there is no chance that they can slip.

**7**

Print the leaves and stems for the ceiling border in the second color.

**8**

Print the stair riser stencil on the wall next to each step. So that you don't print these patterns on an angle (they are somewhat awkward to print), make a mark 3 inches (7.5 cm) above the center of each riser, and then use a level to draw a light horizontal line through the mark. To print, line up the centering marks on the stencil with this horizontal guide line.

**9**

You may wish to put a protective coating over the stair riser motif to guard against heel marks. Ask at your paint store for a nonyellowing finish.

REPEAT

1 SQUARE = 1 INCH

## TRACE AND CUT THE FOLLOWING STENCILS WITH 2-INCH (5 CM) BORDERS:

1. Broken line for chair rail border

2. Circular motif for chair rail border

3. Broken line and flower portion of ceiling border

4. Leaf and stem portion of ceiling border

5. Flower portion of stair riser stencil

6. Leaf portion of stair riser stencil

REPEAT

# CEILING BORDER AND WALL PANEL

*(color pages 89 and 94-95)*

You may combine the ceiling swag, leaves-and-flowers running design, and pineapple included with this project in whatever manner best suits you and the proportions of your room. The running design may be used to make vertical stripes, spaced however you wish in relation to architectural features in the room; it may also be used to frame doors and/or windows. The best way to plan your project is to draw each wall of the room to scale on a piece of graph paper. Include any built-in architectural features, such as openings, chair rails, or fireplaces. Once you have made a "map" of the entire room, draw in the vertical stripes symmetrically spaced on the plan, or place them so that they relate to permanent features (such as a fireplace). Center the pineapples between the stripes. Show the running design around the doors and windows, if you wish.

One of the nice things about stencilling is that when you get near the end of the project, you can look at what is already done and judge whether more should be added. You might like to stencil additional figural elements between the stripes, such as leaves and a small flower or even a willow tree or a peacock. You might also like to add a second border just above the baseboard. If you think the room should have just a little more in it, add any one or more of these. If you think the room is getting a little busy, stop stencilling!

**1**

Prepare the walls as described on page 13.

**2**

If the ceiling is uneven, use a level to draw a straight guide line 2 inches (5 cm) below the ceiling for the ceiling swag (see page14). (If the ceiling is even, you can simply butt the top of the stencil against the ceiling and the 2-inch (5 cm) border will keep the design even.)

**3**

Using your graph paper plan as a guide, mark the walls where vertical patterns should be placed. Use a level to draw light, true vertical lines. Measure for and make small pencil marks to indicate where each pineapple should be placed; use a level to assure that they are aligned horizontally.

**4**

Stencil the ceiling swag. The top of the design should touch the guide line drawn in Step 2. Follow the directions on pages 15-16 for printing continuous borders.

**5**

Center the stencil for the vertical design over the guide lines, and with the same color as used in Step 4, print this continuous design until you reach the baseboard.

**6**

In the second color, print the flower portion of the vertical leaf design.

**7**

Next, apply the pineapple leaves in the first color and then the pineapple in the second color.

STENCILLING A BORDER AROUND A WINDOW

**8**

If you wish, stencil the leaf design around doors and windows. Begin at the top of the window frame on one side of the window and butt the edge of the stencil against the frame to assure a straight border. Stencil down both sides of the window frame, but not above or below it. The width of these side borders determines how far out the stencilling across the top and bottom of the window should go. At the top of the window, place the leaf stencil so that the pattern at the left end of the stencil is even with the outside of the stencil print running down the left side of the window frame. (See illustration at left.) Stencil across the top of the window until the border is even with the outside of the print on the right side of the frame. In the same manner, stencil a border at the bottom of the window. Apply the flower portion of this design.

**9**

Doorways may be treated the same way as the windows. Stencil the sides first; then do the top.

## TRACE AND CUT THE FOLLOWING STENCILS WITH 2-INCH (5 CM) BORDERS:

1. Ceiling swag

2. Leaves and stems for vertical leaf design

3. Flowers for vertical leaf design

4. Pineapple  leaves

5. Pineapple

1 SQUARE = 1 INCH

REPEAT

X

REPEAT

X

# STRAWBERRY BORDER AND FRUIT BOUQUETS FOR A KITCHEN

PLACING AN ANGLED DESIGN IN THE CORNER

Kitchens have many spots you can enliven with stencilling. A ceiling border, cupboards (either natural finish or painted), window and doorway surrounds, even the space between the countertops and the cupboards — all offer opportunities for stencil decoration. You can start with just the ceiling border and keep adding touches until taste dictates that you have enough.

**1**

Prepare the walls and any other surfaces upon which you plan to stencil.

**2**

Run a level along the ceiling to determine if it is relatively even. If it is, you can use the edge of your stencil as a guide for applying the strawberry border. If not, use the level to draw a line 2 inches (5 cm) down from the ceiling; the top of the stencil design (*not* the edge of the stencil) will be placed along this line.

**3**

Following the directions for stencilling continuous designs on pages 15-16, print the strawberry ceiling border. Use one color for the leaves and broken line, and a second color for the strawberries.

**4**

To stencil the small strawberry border around door frames, start on the left side at the floor level, and stencil only until you are even with the top of the frame. For the next design, tilt the stencil on a diagonal, and stencil only one strawberry leaf. For the next design, hold the stencil horizontally and continue over the top of the door (see illustration above). When you come to the other corner, slant the stencil on a diagonal again, stencil one leaf, and then start down the other side of the door from the top to the bottom. Stencil the strawberries in the second color.

**5**

Follow this same procedure for stencilling around windows. If you stencil under the window, make the turn at the corners just as at the top.

**6**

The cupboard design runs vertically down the center of the cupboard doors. Draw a light line down the center of the door. Next, measure the length of the door, and subtract from it the length of the stencil design. Divide your answer in half to get the number of inches from the top of the door the design should begin. Place the top of the leaf stencil design on that mark, and tape the stencil in place, positioning the center marks on the stencil over your pencil guide line. Print the stencil on each of the cupboard doors.

**7**

Print the strawberries, grapes, and pears — each in a different color. Though none of these stencils is large, plan a lot of time for the brush to dry before each color change, unless you have extra brushes.

**8**

You may wish to stencil a strawberry border along the hems of your curtains. (See pages 103-4 for directions on how to stencil on fabric.)

1 SQUARE = 1 INCH

REPEAT

**TRACE AND CUT THE FOLLOWING STENCILS WITH 2-INCH (5 CM) BORDERS:**

1. Leaves and broken line for ceiling border

2. Strawberries for ceiling border

3. Leaves for small border

4. Strawberries for small border

5. Leaves for cupboard design

6. Strawberries for cupboard design

7. Grapes for cupboard design

8. Pears for cupboard design

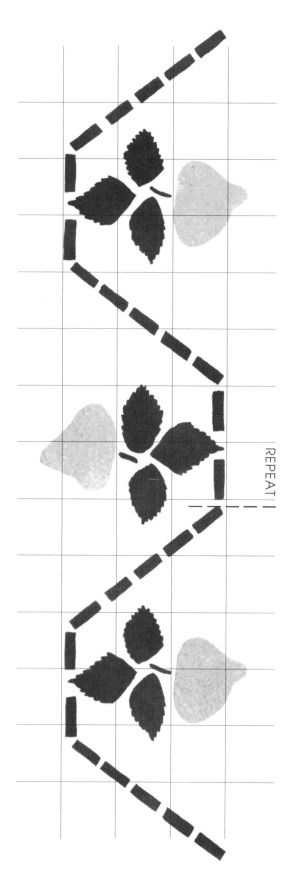

REPEAT

X

X

# FRUIT BORDER AND STRIPES FOR A DINING ROOM

*(color pages 90-91)*

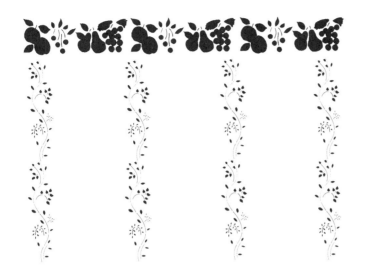

This fruit border can be done in very subtle, light hues on an almost-white background, or it can be made very colorful by painting each type of fruit in its natural shade. Directions will be given for five colors, but you may wish to simplify if it suits your room better.

**1**

Draw a light line all around the room 9 inches (22 cm) down from the ceiling for the fruit border. Use a level while you are measuring, and adjust the line, if necessary, to be sure it is even.

**2**

Plan the placement of the vertical stripes, which should be spaced approximately 36 inches (90 cm) apart. Measure the distance around your room in inches (centimeters), and divide by 36 (90). If the result is not even, calculate how much closer together or farther apart you must place the stripes to achieve regular spacing throughout. Make marks for the verticals just below the line for the ceiling border, and use a level to draw light guide lines for these stripes.

**3**

Beginning in one corner of the room, position the stencil of the leaves for the ceiling border with the center line of the design (*not* the edge of the stencil) on the guide line drawn in step 1. Follow the instructions on pages 15-16 for printing continuous borders, and proceed until the border is complete. Clean the brush and let it dry thoroughly before starting on the next color.

**4**

The fruits may be stenciled in any order. Use the registration marks to place them accurately. Stencil all prints of a fruit throughout the border before moving on to the next fruit; clean and dry your brush between color changes.

**5**

Stencil the vertical design. Tape the stencil in place, taking care to center it along your guide line. This design, like the ceiling border, runs continuously.

## TRACE AND CUT THE FOLLOWING STENCILS WITH 2-INCH (5 CM) BORDERS:

1. Leaves for fruit border

2. Grapes for fruit border

3. Pears for fruit border

4. Apples and cherries for fruit border

5. Vertical stripe

1 SQUARE = 1 INCH

X

REPEAT

X

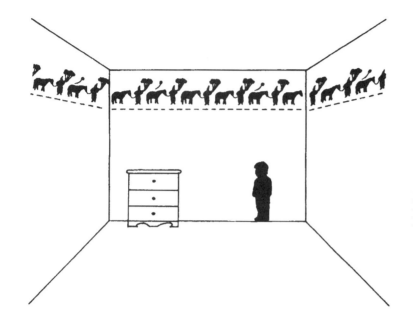

If you use only two or three pastel shades for this design, the effect will be dainty and subdued; if you use a different bright color for each of the three stencils, on the other hand, it will be bright and cheerful.

## MATERIALS

Flat wall paint

Two 12" x 18" (30 cm x 45 cm) stencil sheets and cutting tool

Yardstick and level

Stencil paints

Stencil brush

Paint tray

Scrap paper

Paint thinner and clean cloths

3-inch-wide (7.5 cm) masking tape, gummed on one half

1-inch-wide (2.5 cm) masking tape

Small, short-napped trim roller

**1**

Prepare and paint the walls.

**2**

Measure down from the ceiling 12 inches (30 cm) in several places. Put a level along your measuring marks to determine whether a line drawn between them is exactly horizontal; if it isn't, adjust the marks so it is. Continue the line around the room.

**3**

Your child may find it fun to have his or her silhouette painted on the wall. Have the child stand between a strong light source and the wall, so that you can trace the shadow on the wall. You might like to stencil a bunch of balloons held in the child's hand to match the clowns' balloons.

**4**

Plan the spacing for the clowns along the ceiling border. Starting in one corner, measure the distance around the room. If you made a mark every foot (30 cm), would you come out even? If not, adjust accordingly so that the designs are evenly spaced, *about* 12 inches (30 cm) apart. Try to avoid having a design in a corner. Once you have decided how far apart to place the stencils, make marks for them 1 inch (2.5 cm) up from the border line.

**5**

Stencil a broken line along the guide line drawn in Step 2. To make the broken line, apply masking tape along the line, with the ungummed edge toward the ceiling. Apply another line of tape ¾ inch (1.9 cm) below the first, ungummed edge facing down. Every 2 inches (5cm), place a piece of 1-inch-wide (2.5 cm) masking tape across the stripe to make the breaks in the line. With the trim roller, paint between the lines of the tape.

## 6

Center and print the clown stencil on each of the marks 1 inch (2.5 cm) above the broken line.

## 7

Stencil the pony 1 inch (2.5 cm) above the broken line also. Position the pony so that the lead comes to the clown's hand.

## 8

Stencil the balloons. If you want more balloons in the bunch, add them — in other colors, if you wish. If you want one flying away, stencil it in separately, and use a marking pen to draw in the string flying along behind it.

1 SQUARE = 1 INCH

**TRACE AND CUT THE FOLLOWING STENCILS WITH 2-INCH (5 CM) BORDERS:**

1. Clown

2. Pony

3. Balloon and strings

Although bathrooms are sometimes difficult to stencil because they have so many corners around which to work, this narrow design is long enough to fold around these hard-to-paint places. When you must use a stencil around a corner, you may wish to tape it in several places to keep it flat and stationary.

## MATERIALS

Flat oil-based wall paint

Two 12" x 18" (30 cm x 45 cm) stencil sheets and cutting tool

Measuring tool and level

Stencil paint (2 colors)

Stencil brush

Paint tray

Scrap paper

Paint thinner and clean cloths

**1**

Prepare the walls and apply the background paint.

**2**

Measure down from the ceiling 6 inches (15 cm) in several places. Put a level along the marks to determine whether a line drawn between them is exactly horizontal. Adjust, if necessary, and continue to draw a light line all around the room.

**3**

With the top of the leaves touching the guide line, stencil the leaves and stems, beginning in a place where any mismatch at the start and finish won't be noticeable. Follow the suggestions on pages 15-16 for stencilling continuous borders. Stencil all around the room.

**4**

Use the same border to stencil around the door frame. Print the border on both sides of the door until the design is even with the top of the frame. Position the stencil on both sides so that the flowers will be right side up. For the door top, place the left end of the stencil design (*not* the edge of the stencil sheet) even with the left outside edge of the vertical stencil design. Stencil across the door and stop at the right edge of the vertical stencilled design at the right of the door, even if you are in the middle of a design.

**5**

Place two or three designs on either side of the medicine cabinet, if you wish. To center the design top to bottom, measure the length of the cabinet, subtract the length of the design, and divide that answer in half. The result is the distance down from the top you should begin. Stencil the other side to correspond.

**6**

You may also stencil this border along the baseboard.

**7**

Stencil the blossoms in the second color. Locate the registration marks to place the flower exactly right.

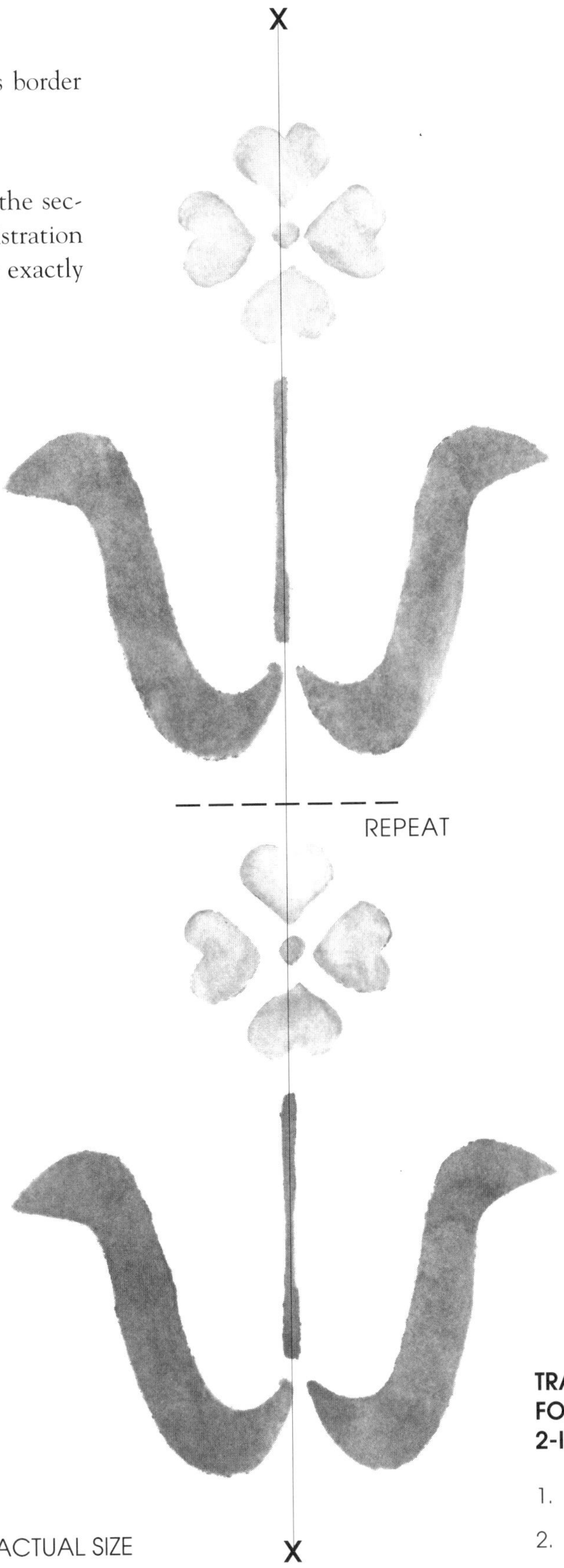

X

REPEAT

**TRACE AND CUT THE FOLLOWING STENCILS WITH 2-INCH (5 CM) BORDERS:**

1. Leaves and stems

2. Blossoms

ACTUAL SIZE

X

# SNOWFLAKE BORDER AND FLEUR-DE-LIS STRIPES FOR A BEDROOM

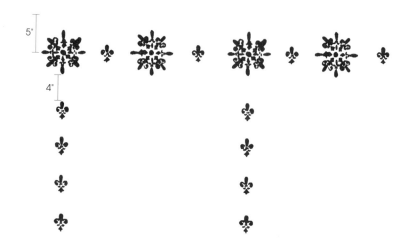

Fleur-de-lis stripes drop from a border of stencilled snowflakes that encircle the room just below the ceiling.

## MATERIALS

Flat wall paint

Four 12" x 18" (30 cm x 45 cm) stencil sheets and cutting tool

Measuring tool and level

Stencil paint (3 colors)

Paint tray

Stencil brush

Scrap paper

Paint thinner and clean cloths

**1**

Prepare the walls and paint them with two coats of the flat paint you have chosen for the background color.

**2**

Measure down from the ceiling 5 inches (13 cm) in several places. Put a level along your measuring marks to determine whether a line drawn between them is exactly level. Adjust, if necessary, and draw a light pencil line all the way around the room.

**3**

Place the center circle and fleur de lis of the border stencil so that the center line of the stencil is on the guide line. Print this design around the room, following the suggestions on pages 15-16 for applying continuous borders.

**4**

With the second color, print the outer portion of the snowflake.

**5**

Print the inner portion of the snowflake with the third color.

**6**

The fleur-de-lis stripe should be stencilled underneath *every other* snowflake design. Find the center snowflake on each wall and use a level as a guide to draw light pencil lines from this point on the border to the baseboard.

**7**

Starting 4 inches (10 cm) below the bottom of the snowflake, print the fleur-de-lis stripe, centered on the guide line. Use the first color (as in Step 3) for this stencil.

**TRACE AND CUT THE
FOLLOWING STENCILS WITH
2-INCH (5 CM) BORDERS:**

1. Center circle of snowflake and fleur-de-lis for ceiling border

2. Outer portion of snowflake for ceiling border

3. Inner portion of snowflake for ceiling border

4. Fleur-de-lis stripe

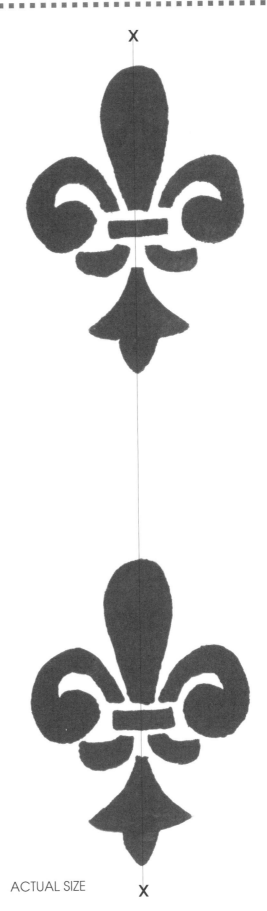

X

ACTUAL SIZE                X

1 SQUARE = 1 INCH

REPEAT

X

X

The focal point of this design is an improvised bouquet in the stylized coal scuttle stencilled over the fireplace mantel. We suggest using one color for the broken stripe of the ceiling border and stencils 1, 3, 4, and 5; a second color for stencils 2 and 6; and a third accent color for stencil 7.

## MATERIALS

Flat or satin-finish wall paint

Six 12" x 18" (30 cm x 45 cm) stencil sheets and cutting tool

Measuring tool and level

Stencil paint (3 colors)

Stencil brush

Paint tray

Scrap paper

3-inch-wide (7.5 cm) masking tape, gummed on one half

1-inch-wide (2.5 cm) masking tape

Paint thinner and clean cloths

Adhesive stencil spray (optional)

**1**
Prepare the surface and apply the background paint.

**2**
Measure and make light marks 10 inches (25 cm) down from the ceiling in several places along the wall. With a level, determine if the ceiling is straight. Adjust, if necessary, and make a light pencil line around the room. Make a second line 4¾ inches (12 cm) above the first.

**3**
To make a frame above the fireplace, use a level as a guide to draw a straight line from each corner of the mantel up to the line drawn for the ceiling border. Find the center of this space, and make a mark.

**4**
On either side of the fireplace "frame" created in Step 3, make marks along the ceiling border line every 3 feet (1 m) to the corners of the fireplace wall. At each 3-foot (1 m) mark, use a level as a guide to draw a light pencil line from the border to the baseboard. Continue these lines all the way around the room. When you come to a doorway, draw from the ceiling border to the top of the casing; when you come to a window, draw above it to the border and below it to the baseboard.

**5**
Lay out the broken stripe under the ceiling border with masking tape by placing tape along the pencil line drawn 10 inches (25 cm) below the ceiling, gummed side on the line, ungummed side toward the floor. One-quarter inch (6 mm) above this line, run more tape, gummed side down, ungummed side toward the ceiling. Cut many pieces of 1-inch-wide (2.5 cm) masking tape 2 inches (5 cm) long and paste one *on a diagonal* every 2

inches (5 cm) along the parallel lines of tape to make long, thin, evenly spaced parallelograms. (See illustration below.) Stencil in the broken stripe with a brush.

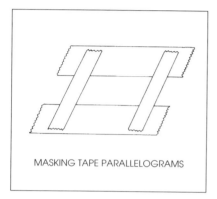

MASKING TAPE PARALLELOGRAMS

**6**

The flowers for the ceiling border should be placed approximately 6 inches (15 cm) apart, but you may need to adjust the spacing so a partial design doesn't end up in a corner. See pages 14-15 for information on how to space a border to avoid this problem. Play with the amount of space between designs until you are satisfied that you will have whole designs in each corner. To indicate placement, make light marks on the upper line drawn in Step 2.

**7**

Position the first stencil for the ceiling border (the stems and leaves) with the center line of the stencil on the upper line drawn in Step 2. Print it all around the room.

**8**

Tape the flower portion of the ceiling border to the wall, matching the registration marks and stencil it around the room.

**9**

Position the stencil for the coal scuttle so the center top of it is on the center mark above the fireplace. Tape the stencil in place so you have a free hand to steady it, since it is rather floppy. Adhesive stencil spray is helpful for this type of stencil.

**10**

Tape and print the stencil for the narrow vertical stripe on each line that frames the area over the fireplace; invert the stencil for the second print so that the leaves run along the outside only. (Follow the instructions on pages 15-16 for printing continuous designs.) Print the same stencil on every other vertical line drawn in Step 4. For each of these stripes *except* the two right above the fireplace opening reverse the stencil and print a second line of leaves on the other side of the broken line (use the broken line for registration).

**11**

On the remaining vertical lines made in Step 4, print the leaves and stems of the wide stripes, again using the continuous design technique. Line up the pattern center marks with the pencilled guide line.

**12**

Stencil the roses and the daisies in the wide stripe.

**13**

Using the same colors for the leaves, roses, and daisies as used in Step 12 for the wide stripe, stencil the floral bouquet over the coal scuttle. Add more flowers here and there, if you wish, to fill and round the bouquet.

## TRACE AND CUT THE FOLLOWING STENCILS WITH 2-INCH (5 CM) BORDERS:

1. Stem and leaves for ceiling border

2. Flower for ceiling border

3. Coal scuttle (for a more stable stencil, cut a separate stencil for the rim and handles, even though they are printed in one color)

4. Leaves and broken line for narrow vertical stripes

5. Leaves and stems for wide vertical stripes

6. Rose blossoms for wide vertical stripes

7. Daisies for wide vertical stripes

8. Leaves and stems for floral bouquet.

9. Rose blossoms for floral bouquet.

10. Daisies for floral bouquet.

X

REPEAT

X

1 SQUARE = 1 INCH

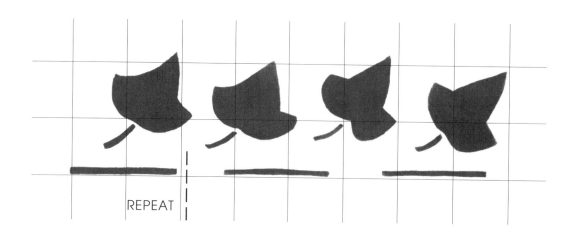

REPEAT

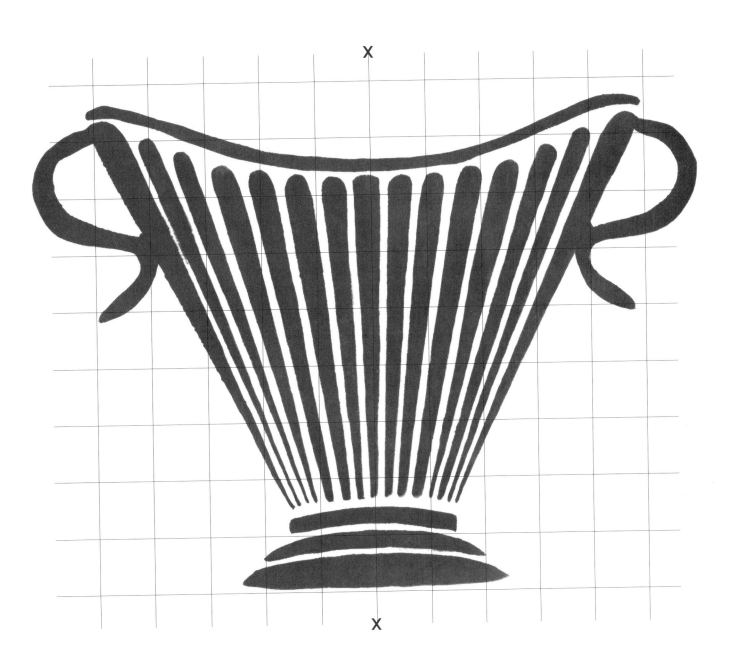

X

X

REGISTRATION MARK ⊕

⊕ REGISTRATION MARK

# ..... CONTEMPORARY GEOMETRICS ....

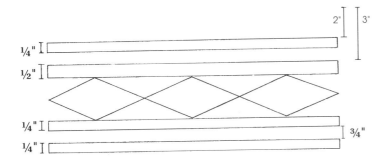

This design is effective executed in either one or several colors. When you trace and cut the stencil, place a metal ruler along the pattern to help you get absolutely straight lines.

**1**
Prepare the wall surface and apply the background paint.

**2**
To make a guide line for the uppermost ¼-inch (6mm) wide stripe, measure down from the ceiling 2 inches (5 cm) in several places. Place the level along the marks to determine if the ceiling is even. Adjust, if necessary, and draw a light pencil line around the room at 2 inches (5 cm). Draw another line 1 inch (2.5 cm) below this as a guide for a ½-inch (1.2 cm) wide stripe.

**3**
For the ¼-inch (6mm) stripe, run masking tape along the upper line, gummed side on the line, ungummed side toward the ceiling. (You will need to fold the top of it over, because it will be too close to the ceiling to lie flat.) One-quarter inch (6mm) below the bottom edge of the tape, run another line of tape, gummed side toward the top tape, ungummed side hanging down. With a brush, paint in the stripe formed by the two pieces of tape.

**4**
As in Step 3, make a second stripe below the first by placing a strip of tape along the lower line and another strip ½ inch (1.2 cm) below it.

**5**
Start the diamond stencil in a corner where any mismatch of the first and last designs will be inconspicuous. Tape the stencil in place, with the top point of the diamond just touching the bottom of the lower stencilled stripe. Position each subsequent diamond so that the point just touches the one printed to the left.

**6**

Use masking tape as in Step 3 to make a ¼-inch (6 mm) wide stripe just touching the bottoms of the diamonds and another ¼-inch (6mm) stripe ¾ inch (1.9 mm) below it.

**7**

In the same manner, stencil a ½-inch (1.2 cm) stripe just above the baseboard, and either one ½-inch (1.2 cm) stripe or a ½-inch (1.2 cm) and a ¼-inch (6mm) stripe around

X                                                          X

ACTUAL SIZE

**TRACE AND CUT THE DIAMOND STENCIL, WITH A 2-INCH (5 CM) BORDER ALL AROUND.**

# 3 STENCILLING FLOORS

A stencilled floor is a real attention-getter. It is somewhat unusual and often regarded difficult, yet it costs little in comparison with buying a rug, cleans easily, wears well, and looks beautiful. Even plywood and other sheet building goods look fine when painted and stencilled. Whether you stencil a geometric design in sharply contrasting colors for a stunning contemporary look, or choose traditional stencil patterns and colors, such a project is well worth the effort.

Instead of stencilling an entire floor, you may wish to stencil a simulated "area rug," centered on the floor or placed where furniture is grouped. You can make this any size, color, or shape — rectangular, circular, oval, even hexagonal — you wish. Plan an oriental-style rug with a border around the outside and individual designs filling the center, or make a simple, regularly spaced geometric design. The design for the Flower-Studded Floor Cloth (pages 52-54) could be used for this purpose.

## PREPARING THE SURFACE

Most floors already have a finish on them, so you must first decide whether to remove the finish or stencil over it. Although removing it means hiring someone or renting floor-sanding equipment and sanding it yourself, a well-prepared surface means that your paint is less likely to chip.

Whether you paint the floor or apply a clear finish so that the natural wood grain shows through, the initial preparations are the same. In either case, consult with your paint dealer to be sure that the base coat you use will accept both your stencil paint and the final protective finish coats you must apply after you stencil. For a painted floor, apply undercoater and two coats of background paint — preferably flat or satin finish; shiny surfaces tend to resist further coats of finish. You need not use floor-and-deck enamel, since you will be coating the entire floor with polyurethane to protect the stencilling. Sand lightly, vacuum, and use a tack cloth between each coat. Don't skip the sanding between coats: the finish will be noticeably nicer if you observe this step. If the background color is to be natural wood grain, apply two coats of clear finish following product directions. After stencilling and before applying the protective finish, go over the whole floor with a tack cloth again to get up every bit of dust and sawdust.

Stencilling may also be done over a previously painted or clear-finished floor without removing the finish completely, if it is in good condition. To prevent chipping, sand the floor lightly, vacuum thoroughly, and use a tack cloth to take up any dust or dirt the vacuum cleaner missed. Apply two coats of background color, being sure to get plenty of paint or finish in the cracks. Sand between coats and pick up residue with a vacuum cleaner and a tack cloth.

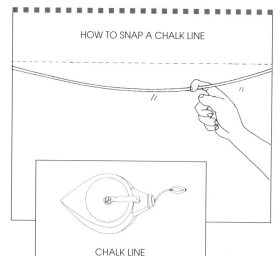

HOW TO SNAP A CHALK LINE

CHALK LINE

## CHOOSING A COLOR

Any color may be used as background color on a stencilled floor, although white or off-white shows dirt and scratches more. When you use a light background color, you must be particularly careful that whatever protective coat you use on the floor after you stencil doesn't turn the base coat yellow (this is not usually a problem with dark colors).

## PLANNING THE DESIGN

Leave at least a 3-inch (7.5 cm) border around the outside edges of the room. A stencilled 12- to 14-inch (30 to 35 cm) wide running border around the entire room with an all-over stencil pattern inside it is quite effective.

For best results, before you begin, draw out the floor and the whole design on a piece of graph paper. If you plan a border, draw it in first, and then plan how to space the design for the center section. Diamond-shaped enclosures can surround a single, central design; stencil designs can be centered within regularly spaced squares or circles. Play with your design on graph paper; wonderful ideas can result.

## MEASURING FOR A STENCILLED FLOOR

When your paper plan is complete, you are ready to measure and mark the border on the floor. Find the center of the room by placing marks on the floor at the exact center of each of the four walls and using a chalk line to connect the opposing marks. (*To use a chalk line*, have an assistant hold the chalk box at the center mark of one wall, while you take the string across the room and place the end on the mark indicating the center of the opposite wall. Holding the chalk-filled string taut with each end on the floor, snap the string on the floor by raising it straight up 6 inches (15 cm) or so at one point along its length and letting go. (See illustration at left.) Where the lines intersect is the center of the room. Verify that these lines intersect at 90-degree angles (see page 8). If a design is off by only a little in the center of a large room, it will be off by several inches by the time the outside of the room is reached.

Once you are sure the center lines intersect at exact right angles, measure out from them to make a grid according to your plan. For instance, if you want to place circles spaced 10 inches (25 cm) apart, snap chalk lines every 10 inches (25 cm). Stop the grid at the lines you made for the border. With a pencil, make a small X at each intersection, and wipe off the chalk lines.

## MAKING STRIPES

A nice technique for setting off the outside border from the rest of the stencilling is to outline it with stencilled stripes. To make the "stencil" for the stripes, use 3-inch-wide (7.5 cm) masking tape or painting tape (a kraft paper designed for this purpose) that is gummed on one half and ungummed on the other. For a 1-inch (2.5 cm) stripe, lay down strips of masking tape 1 inch (2.5 cm) apart, with the gummed halves of the masking tape facing inward, so that paint can't run under the tape. Measure the spacing between the tapes carefully; once the lines are painted, mistakes will be obvious. When you reach a corner, cut the tape, and continue with a new piece at right angles to the tape already in place. (See illustration at right.)

Use a small, short-napped trim roller to apply paint in the space between the two strips of masking tape. (Paint may also be applied with a stencil brush, but it will take longer.) Before removing the tape, check places where the line goes across cracks between the floorboards. If there are breaks in the color because paint didn't go into the cracks far enough, use a small artist's brush to paint color into the cracks. When you peel the tape away, you should have perfectly straight stripes.

## APPLYING THE DESIGN

Stencil designs are applied to a floor in the same way as to walls, except that care must be taken with the cracks. To avoid paint buildup on the edges of the cracks, use a very dry brush, or a trim roller with a short nap. Plan the order in which you will work, starting at the farthest point away from the door and painting toward the door — you don't want to paint yourself in! You may find that you can't work on a floor too long at one time, both because you tire in the squatting position you must assume when you paint and because you must let each stencil pattern dry completely before you can get on the floor to add another color.

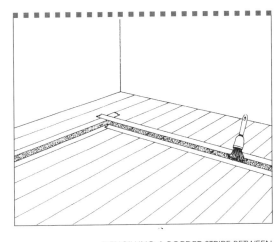

STENCILLING A BORDER STRIPE BETWEEN LINES OF MASKING TAPE. NOTE HOW TAPE IS CUT TO FORM THE CORNER.

## PRESERVING YOUR WORK

When the design is thoroughly dry — dry enough to walk on without any sticking — apply two coats of finish (polyurethane, for example) over it to preserve it. If your base coat is white or cream color, ask your paint dealer for suggestions of what to use to preserve the stencilling without risk of yellowing the design or the background color.

# ALL-OVER FLORAL DESIGN FOR A FLOOR

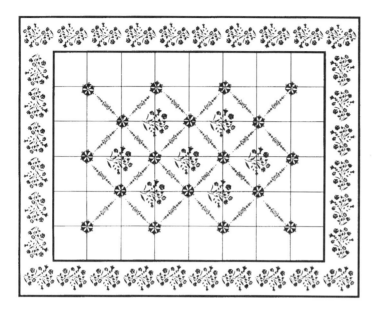

This design is created by first encircling the room with a double-striped border, within which is a stencilled continuous design. A circular design marks the four corners of a latticelike, all-over pattern that fills the center of the room.

## MATERIALS

Wood primer

Flat or satin-finish background paint

Polyurethane

5 sheets 80-grit sandpaper, sanding block, and tack cloth or chamois

Seven 12" x 18" (30 cm x 45 cm) stencil sheets and cutting tool

Measuring tools and chalk box

Stencil paint (2 colors)

Stencil brush or short-napped trim roller

Paint tray

Scrap paper

3-inch-wide (7.5 cm) masking tape, gummed on one half

Paint thinner and clean cloths

**1**

Prepare the floor as described on pages 45-46.

**2**

Find the center of the room and divide it in half with exactly perpendicular lines. From these center lines, mark a 1-foot (30 cm) grid with the chalk line (see page 46). Carry the grid to within about 6 inches (15 cm) of the baseboard all around. Mark each intersection of the grid with a small pencil mark, and wash off the chalk lines. (Paint doesn't adhere well to dusty surfaces.)

**3**

Using the technique described on page 47, make a guide for the first border stripe by running two lines of masking tape ½ inch (1.2 cm) apart, sticky sides toward the stripe, on the last line of the grid, about 6 inches (15 cm) from the walls. If a hearth or closet projects into the

room, bring the stripe out around it, keeping the 6-inch spacing constant.

Mix the color for the stripe, and with a brush or roller, apply it in the space between the tapes. If paint does not fill in cracks where the stripe crosses floorboards, use a small artist brush to paint it in. Don't paint over areas already covered, because the color in the stripe will not be even if you do. Lift the tape. If any paint went under the tape, remove it with paint thinner on a clean cloth. Stencil another stripe on the next grid line 1 foot (30 cm) away from the first.

**4**

Stencil the running border centered between the parallel lines created in Step 3. Measure and mark the center of the space between the stripes, and align this center with the registration marks on the stencil. Start stencilling the leafy part of the border in the least visible corner of the room. Follow the suggestions on pages 15-16 for stencilling continuous borders. When you approach a corner, leave enough space to turn the corner and keep the border centered between the stripes. Continue the design all the way around the room. Stencil right up to the point where you began (be careful not to stencil over it). Clean the brush and the stencil, and take a break to rest your back!

## 5

Stencil the flowers for the border.

## 6

The circular design that marks the four corners of each diamond is placed every other foot (30 cm) on the 1-foot (30 cm) grid. Find the first row of markings 1 foot (30 cm) inside the border stripe, and starting at a corner, stencil the first circular design on a mark. Working parallel to one border, skip the next 1-foot (30 cm) mark, and place a circular design *every other mark*, until you reach the border at the other side of the room. Next, go back to the corner where you began, and stencil in the circles along the border at right angles to your first row. The first design on this row is the first one you stencilled; stencil *every other mark* until the design is printed up to the far border. When you begin your third row, *be sure to skip the first mark*; so that this row is staggered from the first row (see illustration).

## 7

Stencil the linear design diagonally across the grid, connecting the circular designs. (When all of these are in place, each diamond should have one pencil mark at its center; this is the center mark for the central motif.)

## 8

In the center of each diamond, stencil the central motif. (This part of the design is optional. If you prefer a more open design, leave this one out.)

## 9

To preserve the stencilling, apply two coats of polyurethane over the entire floor, following the product directions for treatment between coats; usually a light sanding and picking up the residue with a vacuum cleaner and tack cloth is recommended. A satin finish makes a nice final coat.

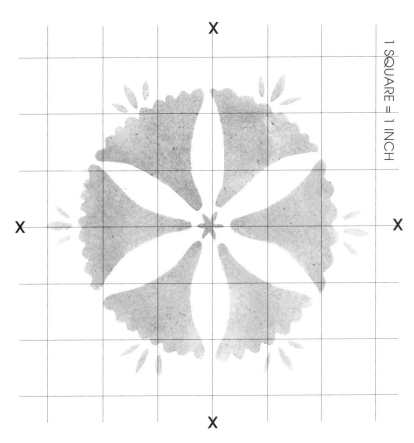

1 SQUARE = 1 INCH

**TRACE AND CUT THE FOLLOWING STENCILS WITH 2-INCH (5 CM) BORDERS:**

1. Leaves for border

2. Flowers for border

3. Circular design for corners

4. Linear design that connects corners

5. Leaves for central motif

6. Flowers for central motif

REPEAT

# FLOWER-STUDDED FLOOR CLOTH

*(color page 89)*

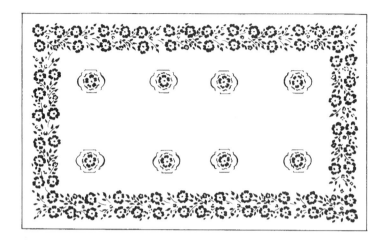

Since American colonial days, inexpensive rugs known as "floor cloths" have been made by painting heavyweight canvas and applying a stencilled design. Floor cloths may be cut and stitched to any size or shape needed. The canvas receives three coats of paint before it is stencilled. The paint fills the roughness of the canvas to make a nice surface for stencilling, and it also creates a surface easily wiped clean with soap and water.

Hem the canvas all around before painting. Because canvas is bulky, turn the edge only once, and seal the raw edges on the back with paint.

**1**

To prepare the canvas, iron it, and then paint it with three coats of the background paint, allowing each coat to dry thoroughly before you apply the next. When the paint is dry, iron it again, using a pressing cloth to protect the paint.

**2**

Since the design is most easily applied to a grid, draw light pencil lines 1 foot (30 cm) apart in each direction. Use a carpenter's square to make sure that each of the blocks is perfectly square; the design is regular and should have a geometric appearance when completed.

**3**

Print the leaves and flower centers for the border. Place the edge of the stencil against the edge of the canvas with the design 2 inches (5 cm) from the edge. Start in the upper left-hand corner. Be sure to begin and end the stencil design 2 inches (5 cm) from the ends of the rug; make small marks 2 inches (5 cm) away from all edges as reminders. Stencil along one edge in the first color, following the suggestions on pages 15-16 for stencilling continuous borders. When you reach the 2-inch (5 cm) mark at the end of the rug, stop, move the stencil to the opposite side of the rug, and stencil a line that parallels the first one. Be sure to place the same edge of the stencil along the outside edge of the rug on both sides; otherwise, the border will print upside down. Begin and end this border 2 inches (5 cm) inside the ends of the rug, and then stencil along the two ends of the rug inside the two side borders. Remember to position the stencil with the same edge facing out.

**4**

Print the first stencil for the central motifs — the flower center and frame — with the same color as the border leaves. Place the flower center on the intersections of the grid, and align the center line with the grid lines. The straight edges of the frame should be parallel with the sides of the rug.

**5**

Print the border with the second color.

**6**

With the same color, print the remaining central motifs. Allow the prints to dry completely.

**7**

To make the rug durable, apply three coats of polyurethane over the design, following product directions for advice on how to apply the second and third coats. The polyurethane may need to be sanded between coats to make the second and third coats stick to the

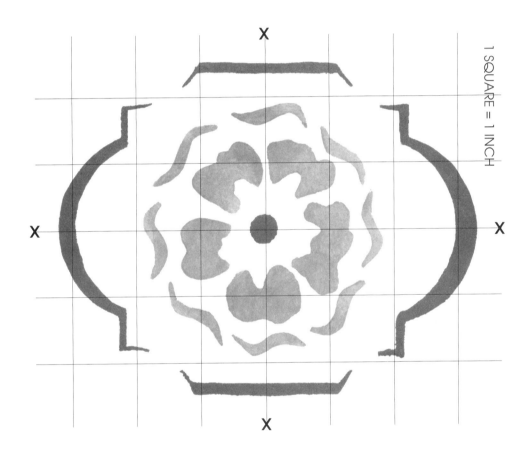

X

X

X

X

1 SQUARE = 1 INCH

**TRACE AND CUT THE FOLLOWING STENCILS WITH 2-INCH (5 CM) BORDERS:**

1. Leaves and flower centers for border

2. Flowers for border

3. Outer frame and flower center for central motif

4. Remainder of geometric motif

X

REPEAT

X

# 4 STENCILLING ON WOOD

## FURNITURE AND HOUSEHOLD ACCESSORIES

Unfinished furniture stores, secondhand or antique shops, and your own attic or basement are all likely places to seek out furniture appropriate for stencilling. Before you spend the time and effort to stencil a piece, be sure to make any necessary repairs and prepare the surface thoroughly and carefully.

Stencilling is attractive on both painted and natural wood finishes. In either case, before you apply any new coats of paint or sealer, remove hardware, and completely strip off all old paint or varnish. You may have the piece "dipped" commercially or remove the finish yourself. If you do it yourself, be careful not to get too much water on the piece when you wash off the remover. Old glues tend not to hold up, and on chairs, in particular, joints may be weakened and require regluing. If you plan to repaint the piece, it is not essential to get every bit of paint out of the joints, but do prepare a good working surface — you want your piece to be both hardy and handsome.

Whether you are working with old furniture that has been stripped, or new, unfinished furniture, sand the entire surface lightly, using increasingly fine sandpaper as the surface becomes smooth. (Sandpaper is sold in a variety of degrees of roughness, called "grit." The higher the grit number, the finer the paper. You may wish to use 80 for rough sanding, 150 for semi-finishing, and 220 for fine sanding.) For flat surfaces, you will find it easier to sand if you wrap your sandpaper around a block of wood. Vacuum up the residue, and wipe the surface with a tack cloth or chamois to pick up any remaining dust. If you are going to paint the piece, apply a primer; if you plan a natural wood finish, apply a coat of wood sealer. Allow the base coat to dry thoroughly, and then sand the piece with 220-grit sandpaper. For painted furniture, apply two coats of the background paint, sanding between coats and picking up the residue as described above.

## MATERIALS

80-, 150-, 220-grit
sandpaper, sanding
block, and tack cloth or
chamois

½ pint (¾ litre) primer

1 pint (1 litre) flat paint

One 9" x 12" (23 cm x 30
cm) and two 12" x 18" (30
cm x 45 cm) stencil sheets
and cutting tool

Measuring tool

Stencil paint (2 colors)

Stencil brush

Paint tray

Scrap paper

Paint thinner and clean
cloths

½ pint (¾ litre) satin-finish
polyurethane

Bureaus offer many possibilities for creative decoration. The piece may be painted or left with the natural wood grain showing; the stencilled design may be done with paint or metallic powder (see pages 85-86). Stencil designs may be placed in the middle of each drawer; a small border may be run around each corner of the top of the bureau to complement the drawer stencil; the bottom, side panels, and even legs can be decorated. One of the advantages of stencilling is that you can start printing designs in the obvious places and keep adding until you feel you've done enough. On furniture, in particular, little bits of stencilling can be tucked here and there, and the result is likely to be successful.

This design consists of a two-color stencil at the center of the drawers, a small, two-color running border on the stretchers between drawers and on the end panels, and a one-color running border to frame the top. If there is room you may also run the two-color border on the panels above and below the drawers, and down the front side panels.

Before stencilling, remove all hardware and refinish the piece. Bureaus take a lot of heavy wear, and drawers in particular are likely to be chipped. Sand the piece until it is smooth, and pick up the residue with a vacuum cleaner and tack cloth. Follow the suggestions on page 55 for refinishing.

**1**

Prepare the bureau for painting, and apply primer and two coats of the background color, sanding lightly between coats. (See page 55 for further suggestions.)

**2**

Tip the bureau on its back and use the leaves-and-tulips design to stencil the stretchers between the drawers, and, if you wish, the panels above and below the drawers and the vertical front side panels. Follow the instructions on pages 15-16 for stencilling continuous borders. Fill the stretcher space completely, left to right; center the border on the panels above and below the drawers; and place the vertical stencilling on the side panels as close to the inside edges as possible, so that the borders form a continuous design above, below, between, and beside the drawers.

Be sure to place the tulips so that they are "growing up" on the vertical borders and always facing the same direction on the horizontal borders.

**3**

Stencil the tulips-and-leaves border around the side panels. If possible, tip the bureau on its side so that you have a flat surface on which to work.

**4**

To stencil the drawers, pull them out of the bureau, and stand them on their backs, so you have a flat surface on which to work. Mark the center of each drawer, and draw a light pencil line horizontally along the center. Center the leaf stencil on the mark and align the center line along the horizontal. Tape the stencil in place and print it on each drawer.

**5**

Print the simple border for the top first from the left corners to the right at both front and back. Use the edge of the stencil as a guide to place the design 2 inches (5 cm) from the front and back edges. Tape this stencil in place while you are working. Print the border on the sides between the front and back borders.

**6**

Protect your work with a coat of satin-finish polyurethane. Stir it well before you spread it on and very frequently as you work, or it will streak. Try to keep dust away from it while it is drying. Wait until the final coat of polyurethane is completely dry before you replace the drawer pulls, so that you don't scratch the finish.

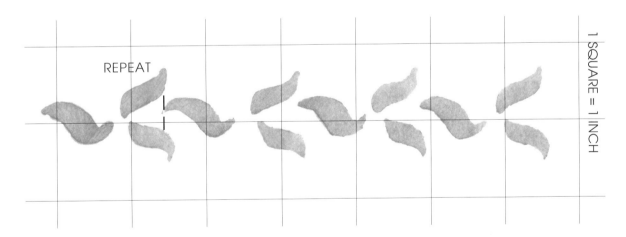

REPEAT

1 SQUARE = 1 INCH

**TRACE AND CUT THE FOLLOWING STENCILS WITH 1½-INCH (4 CM) BORDERS:**

1. Leaves for two-color running border

2. Tulips for two-color running border

## TRACE AND CUT THE FOLLOWING STENCILS WITH 2-INCH (5 CM) BORDERS:

3. Leaves and stems for drawer center

4. Flowers for drawer center

5. One-color running border for top and sides

REGISTRATION MARK ⊕

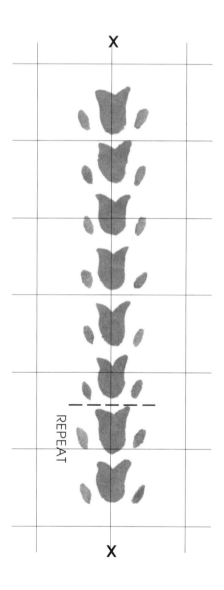

1 SQUARE = 1 INCH

# PENNSYLVANIA DUTCH-STYLE HOPE CHEST

*(color page 94)*

## MATERIALS

A chest

80-, 150-, and 220-grit sandpaper and tack cloth or chamois

½ pint (¾ litre) primer

1 pint (1 litre) flat paint (usually a dark color)

½ pint (¾ litre) off-white paint

Six 12" x 18" (30 cm x 45 cm) stencil sheets plus additional material for panel patterns, and cutting tool

Measuring tools, pencil, and string

Adhesive spray

Stencil paint (3 colors)

Stencil brush

Trim roller with a short nap

Paint tray

Scrap paper

Paint thinner and clean cloths

Stencilling either an old chest or a new, unfinished one can be a very rewarding project. Chests fit into almost any room, whether formal or informal; choose a stencil design most appropriate to your own decorating needs. Like other pieces of furniture, chests may be painted or left with a natural wood finish; the stencilling can be done with paint or metallic powders (see pages 85-86). You may decide to put stencilling only on the top or as a small running border along the edge of the lid, or you may cover the chest with decorative patterns.

Later known as the Pennsylvania Dutch, German and Swiss immigrants who settled in Pennyslvania during the seventeenth and eighteenth centuries developed a distinctive and colorful folk art. This blanket chest, or hope chest, uses some of the popular motifs of this tradition. It is painted in two colors, a dark color for most of the chest, and a light color for the two panels on the front and one on each end. The patterns provided are for a chest 38 inches (96 cm) wide, 22 inches (56 cm) high, and 16 inches (41 cm) deep. You can adjust the sizes and proportions to suit your chest (see page 12 for further information). The figural motifs may be done in whatever colors you wish.

## 1

Remove all hardware on the chest so it won't get paint on it, and prepare the surface as suggested on page 55. Apply a coat of primer. Paint the front and ends of the chest with two coats of the off-white color. Allow the paint to dry thoroughly.

## 2

Draw a light vertical line down the center of the front and the two ends of the chest.

**3**

Position the panel patterns on the front of the chest so that the inner edges are 1 inch (2.5 cm) from the center line drawn in Step 2. Center the side panels on each end of the chest. Use adhesive spray to affix the patterns to the chest while you are painting. Use a trim roller to paint what is *not* covered by the pattern with the dark-colored paint. Allow the paint to dry, and apply a second coat before removing the patterns. At the same time, apply two coats of the dark paint to the lid and back of the chest.

**4**

Draw a light line down the center of each light-colored "panel." Center and print the jug-and-flower stencil on each of the front panels, placing the bottom of the jug 1 inch (2.5 cm) up from the bottom of the panel. Print the design on the right panel first, then clean the stencil on both sides, reverse it, and print the design on the left. In this way, the jug handle will be on the outside on both panels.

**5**

Stencil the leaves and stems on the front panels. Stencil the leaves and stems on the side panels, placing the end of the stem 1 inch (2.5 cm) up from the bottom of the panel and centering the stencil on the guide line.

**6**

Stencil the flowers on the sides with the same color as used for the jug and flowers on the front.

**7**

Stencil the running border around the top, as an outline around each of the panels, and along the edge of each corner. Use the third color for this motif.

**8**

Replace the hardware. Apply a protective coat of paste wax to the whole chest.

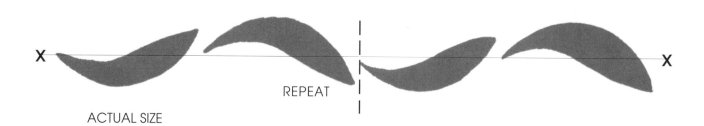

ACTUAL SIZE

REPEAT

**TRACE AND CUT THE FOLLOWING STENCILS WITH 2-INCH (5 CM) BORDERS:**

1. Jug and flowers for front panels

2. Leaves and stems for front panels

3. Leaves and stems for side panels

4. Flowers for side panels

5. Running border

6. On heavy paper (preferably stencil material), trace two copies of each of the panel patterns. Cut the patterns out. You will use these to mask out sections of the front and sides when you apply the main color to the chest.

X

1 SQUARE = 1 INCH

X

X

X

1 SQUARE = 1 INCH

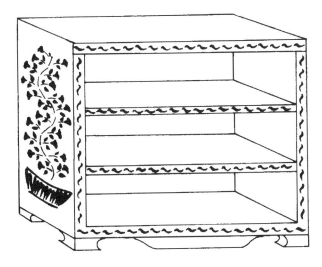

B ecause the patterns for this bookcase are both running designs, they may be adapted to any size bookcase.

## MATERIALS

Bookcase

80-, 150-, 220-grit sandpaper, sanding block, and tack cloth or chamois

Primer and flat paint

Three 12" x 18" (30 cm x 45 cm) stencil sheets and cutting tool

Stencil paint (2 colors)

Stencil brush

Paint tray

Scrap paper

Paint thinner and clean cloths

**1**
Prepare the surface for stencilling as suggested on page 55. Prime the wood, and apply two coats of the background color, sanding lightly with 150-grit sandpaper and cleaning off all sawdust between coats.

**2**
Stencil the narrow running border along all narrow edges — shelves and dividers, top and side edges. Do the verticals first and then the horizontals. It is difficult to stencil such narrow places without moving the stencil, so it's best to tape the stencil down or use adhesive spray to keep it in place while you print. Follow the suggestions on pages 15-16 for printing continuous borders.

**3**
Draw a light, pencil line down the full length of the exact center of both side boards. If possible, tip the bookcase on its side so you can stencil on a horizontal surface. Center the compote at the bottom of the board, tape it down, and stencil it in.

**4**
Position the vine so that it is centered and the bottom of it is as close as possible to the compote rim without touching it. Stencil it in, and then continue stencilling the vine until you reach the top of the bookcase. Use the registration marks to keep the vine centered on the guide line. Finish the vine at the top by printing whole leaves, even if you must "cheat" a bit to do so. Repeat on the other side of the bookcase.

**5**
Print the morning-glories, adding a few at the top, if necessary, to fill out and complete the design.

**6**
When the paint is thoroughly dry, apply a coat of paste wax to the entire bookcase.

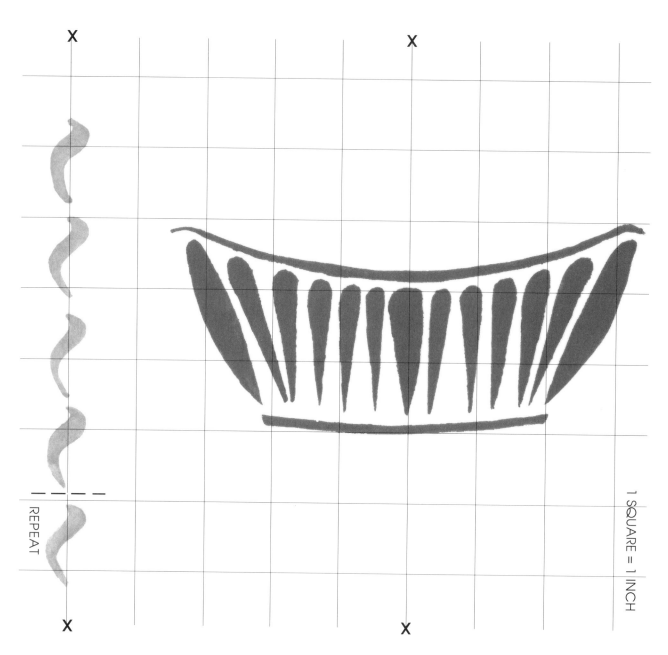

X         X

REPEAT

1 SQUARE = 1 INCH

X         X

**TRACE AND CUT THE FOLLOWING STENCILS WITH 1½-INCH (4 CM) BORDERS:**

1. Figural border

2. Leaves and stems of vine

3. Morning-glories

X

REPEAT

1 SQUARE = 1 INCH

The design for the outside of the head- and footboard panels is a two-color, hearts-and-leaves border; on the inside of the panels two bears sit back to back in a bed of flowers. Be sure to use lead-free paint for this project, or indeed, for any project if you have young children.

## MATERIALS

Crib

80-, 150-, 220-grit sandpaper, sanding block, and tack cloth or chamois

1 pint (1 litre) primer

1 pint (1 litre) background color paint

Four 12" x 18" (30 cm x 45 cm) stencil sheets and cutting tool

Measuring tool

Stencil paint (3 colors, green for the leaves and stems, brown for the bear and cattails, and a third color of your choice)

Stencil brush

Paint tray

Scrap paper

**1**
Prepare the crib for stencilling as suggested on page 55.

**2**
Make the following guide marks for placement of designs: For the border design on the outside of the head- and footboard panels, draw a line 2 inches (5 cm) in from the edges all the way around. On the inside, locate the centers of these panels and make marks 12 inches (30 cm) down from the top.

**3**
Print the running border on the outside of the head- and footboard panels. Begin at the upper right corner, and place a portion of the curved line that arches out in the corner. Stencil around the entire panel, and at each corner, place a part of the design that arches outward. Use green for the leaves and stems, and whatever color you wish for the hearts.

**4**
With brown, stencil the bears, positioned so that they sit back to back on either side of the center mark. (Reverse the stencil to print a mirror image.)

**5**
Using green, print the leaves and stems in the flower bed around the bears. (This stencil, too, should be reversed to print a mirror image.)

**6**
With brown, print the cattails at the ends of the stems already printed.

**7**
Print the flowers in the third color.

**8**
When the bears are completely dry, stencil their features using a darker shade of brown. (By over-printing with the same brown used for the bear bodies, you may be able to get a dark enough shade.)

## TRACE AND CUT THE FOLLOWING STENCILS WITH 2-INCH (5 CM) BORDERS:

1. Leaves and stems for border
2. Hearts for border
3. Bear
4. Bear's features
5. Leaves and stem
6. Flower blossoms
7. Cattail tops

REGISTRATION MARK

CENTER

1 SQUARE = 1 INCH

REGISTRATION MARK

X                                                                    X

REPEAT

# CHILD'S CHAIR, HIGH CHAIR, OR DOLL'S CHAIR

*(color page 93)*

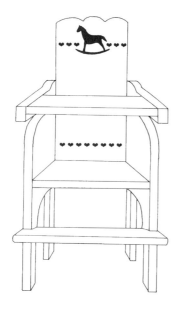

Stencil your child's chair, and then stencil a doll's chair to match. Adjust the size of this design, and the suggested measurements in the instructions, according to the size of the space to be stencilled.

## MATERIALS

A child's chair, high chair, or doll's chair with a back suitable for stencilling

80-, 150-, 220-grit sandpaper and tack cloth or chamois

½ pint (¾ litre) primer

½ pint (¾ litre) flat background paint

One 9" x 12" (23 cm x 30 cm) stencil sheet and cutting tool

Measuring tool

Stencil paint (2 colors)

Stencil brush

Scrap paper

Paint thinner and clean cloths

½ pint (¾ litre) satin-finish polyurethane (optional)

**1**

Prepare the chair for stencilling as suggested on page 55.

**2**

Find the center back of the chair side to side. Make a mark at the center 4 inches (10 cm) down from the top. If you are stencilling a narrow slat, draw a light line all the way across, equidistant from top and bottom; if you are stencilling a solid back, draw a line 3 inches (7.5 cm) down from the top.

**3**

Position the horse on the center line, with the bottom of the rockers on the mark made 4 inches (10 cm) from the top. Tape the stencil in place, and print the design.

**4**

Beginning 1½ (4 cm) inches to the right of the horse, and using a new color, stencil the heart border along the 3-inch (7.5 cm) guide line; place the bottom tips of the hearts on the line. Print the same number of hearts beginning 1½ inches (4 cm) to the left of the horse. Print the hearts wherever else you think they would look nice, depending on the design of the chair.

**5**

Apply a coat of polyurethane for protection.

**TRACE AND CUT THE FOLLOWING STENCILS WITH 2-INCH (5 CM) BORDERS:**

1.  Rocking horse

2.  Hearts

ACTUAL SIZE

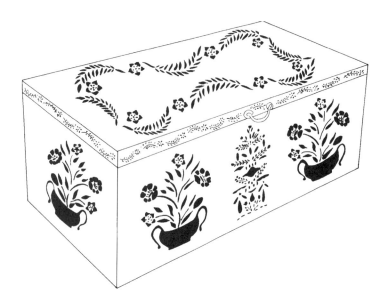

**4**

With the same color, print the vase and leaves on the front and both ends; on the front, center the vase in the spaces on each side of the center front design.

**5**

With the same color, print the leaves of the small running border around the entire top edge.

**6**

Tip the box onto its bottom again, and print the swags for the top. Print the center front swag first, and then balance the others around it. Alternate concave and convex swags, leaving room for a flower between each, and planning the placement so that complete swags may be printed. When you are done, you will have a border of swags around the entire top.

**7**

When the vase is completely dry, apply the decorative shading on it. Use the same color as you used for the vase, but apply it more heavily.

**8**

In the second color, print all of the flowers—in the vases, between the swags, and in the running border.

**9**

Apply a coat of satin-finish polyurethane over the entire toy box for very durable finish. (If you wish, you can wax the box instead.) Put the hardware back on.

## MATERIALS

An unfinished chest

80-, 150-, 220-grit sandpaper, sandpaper block, and tack cloth or chamois

1 pint (1 litre) primer

1 quart (1 litre) flat or satin-finish paint

One 9" x 12" (23 cm x 30 cm) and five 12" x 18" (30 cm x 45 cm) stencil sheets and cutting tool

Measuring tools

Stencil paint (2 colors)

Stencil brush

Paint tray

Scrap paper

Paint thinner and clean cloths

½ pint (¾ litre) polyurethane (optional)

**1**

Remove all hardware, and prepare surface as suggested on page 55. For wide, flat surfaces such as this, your sanding will go faster and be more even if you wrap your sandpaper over a block of wood. Apply one coat of primer, sand lightly, and take up the residue with a vacuum cleaner and tack cloth.

**2**

Mark the centers of the front and both ends of the toybox.

**3**

Turn the box on its back and print the center front design on the center line.

**TRACE AND CUT THE FOLLOWING STENCILS WITH 2-INCH (5 CM) BORDERS:**

1. Center front design

2. Vase and leaves

3. Leaves for small running border

4. Swag

5. Dark shading on vase

6. Blossoms

7. Flower between swags

8. Flowers for small running border

ACTUAL SIZE

ACTUAL SIZE

REPEAT

1 SQUARE = 1 INCH

Stencilling can transform a very ordinary object — such as a sap bucket, a pail, a large plant pot (if there is no hole in the bottom), a plain wooden wastebasket, or even an inexpensive plastic trash container — into a handsome wastebasket.

## MATERIALS

A container suitable for use as a wastebasket

80-, 150-, 220-grit sandpaper (for unfinished wood surfaces only) and tack cloth

Background paint (if necessary)

Two 12" x 18" (30 cm x 45 cm) stencil sheets and cutting tool

Tape measure

Stencil paints (2 colors)

Stencil brush

Paint tray

Scrap paper

Paint thinner and clean cloths

**1**

Prepare the surface for application of the background paint — if wood, sand, prime, and paint; if metal, buff with steel wool, prime, and paint.

**2**

Measure and mark a line around the wastebasket, 2 inches (5 cm) down from the top. Measure and mark a line 2 inches (5 cm) up from the bottom. Mark the centers of the front and back sides of the basket.

**3**

Apply the small running border on the lines at both top and bottom. Follow the suggestions on pages 15-16 for stencilling continuous borders. Make the first print on one of the sides — not on a line with either of the center marks. You probably won't end up with a perfect match when you stencil around to the start, but if you are careful, you can juggle the stencil so you can come close.

**4**

Print the leaf stencil at the center of the wastebasket, on both sides.

**5**

Matching the registration marks, print the flower.

**6**

There is usually no need to apply a protective coating to a wastebasket if you use permanent paints. A coat of wax, however, will prevent any stains from getting on the paint.

## TRACE AND CUT THE FOLLOWING STENCILS WITH 2-INCH (5 CM) BORDERS:

1. Borders for top and bottom

2. Leaves and stem

3. Flowers

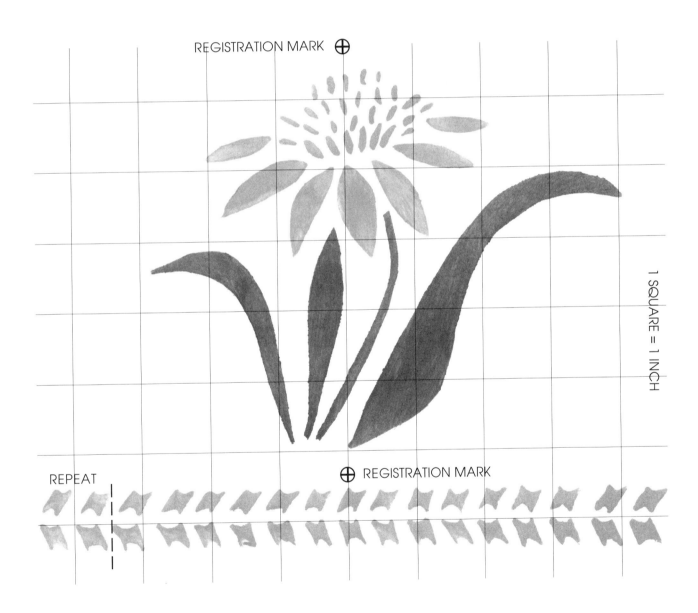

REGISTRATION MARK ⊕

1 SQUARE = 1 INCH

⊕ REGISTRATION MARK

REPEAT

*(color pages 90, 94, and 95)*

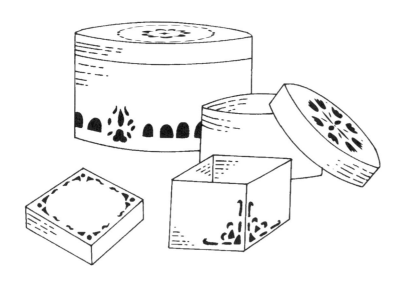

## MATERIALS

Two round and one square wooden box

150- and 220-grit sandpaper and tack cloth

½ pint (¾ litre) flat or satin-finish paint, in a bright color

One 9" x 12" (23 cm x 30 cm) stencil sheet and cutting tool

Stencil paint

Stencil brush

Paint tray

Scrap paper

½ pint (¾ litre) satin-finish polyurethane

Small, wooden household objects make perfect stencil projects, especially for beginners. Your imagination will suggest dozens of objects that can be stencilled to make unique, personalized gifts or family treasures for your own home — in less time than you might imagine. One of the most charming is a stencilled wooden box, which could serve as a jewelry box, recipe box, sewing box, or card box. Large wooden crates, stencilled, make excellent, inexpensive bookcases; for smaller projects, use the wooden boxes in which salt codfish is sold, or the round wooden boxes in which some cheeses are packaged. Most craft stores sell boxes in a variety of sizes and shapes.

Choose stencil patterns in scale with the object being stencilled. In addition to those shown here, many other patterns in this book could be reduced and adapted for this purpose. Either of the corner designs could be used on square or rectangular boxes. Two options for circular or oval boxes are included. The first features a wheel of tulips, which may be used alone or with a border formed by stencilling the small arch of tulips along the outside edge. The second consists of a segmented flower within a circle on the lid and a continuous running border around the side of the box.

**1**

Sand the surface of both boxes and both lids; pick up the residue with a vacuum cleaner and tack cloth. Apply two or three coats of the background paint.

### FOR ROUND OR OVAL BOX 1

**2**

With pencil, draw a light line around the box ¾ in (1.9 mm) from the edge. Find and mark the center of the box lid.

**3**

Print the arch of tulips along the line drawn in Step 2. The rounded part of the arch should almost touch the edge of the box, and the feet of the arch should almost touch each other on the guide line.

**4**

Using two different colors, print the two parts of the circular motif, centered on the lid.

### FOR ROUND OR OVAL BOX 2

**5**

Centering the designs on the lid, print the outer circle in one color and the flower in a second color.

**6**

Print the two stencils for the running border with the bottom of the border about ½ inch (1.2 cm) from the bottom of the box.

### FOR SQUARE OR RECTANGULAR BOX

**7**

With pencil, draw light guide lines in each corner of the lid, ½ inch (1.2 cm) from the edge, for positioning the corner stencils.

**8**

Place the corner stencil along the guide lines drawn in Step 7, and print one design in each corner.

**9**

When the stencil paint is thoroughly dry, apply a protective coat of polyurethane over each box.

X

REGISTRATION MARKS ⊕          ⊕

X

ACTUAL SIZE

**TRACE AND CUT THE FOLLOWING STENCILS WITH 2-INCH (5 CM) BORDERS:**

**For round or oval box 1:**

1. Arch of tulips for border
2. Petals and dots for circular motif
3. Tulips for circular motif

**For round or oval box 2:**

4. Outer circle
5. Flower
6. Part one of running border
7. Part two of running border

**For square or rectangular box:**

8. One of the corner motifs (depending on size of box)

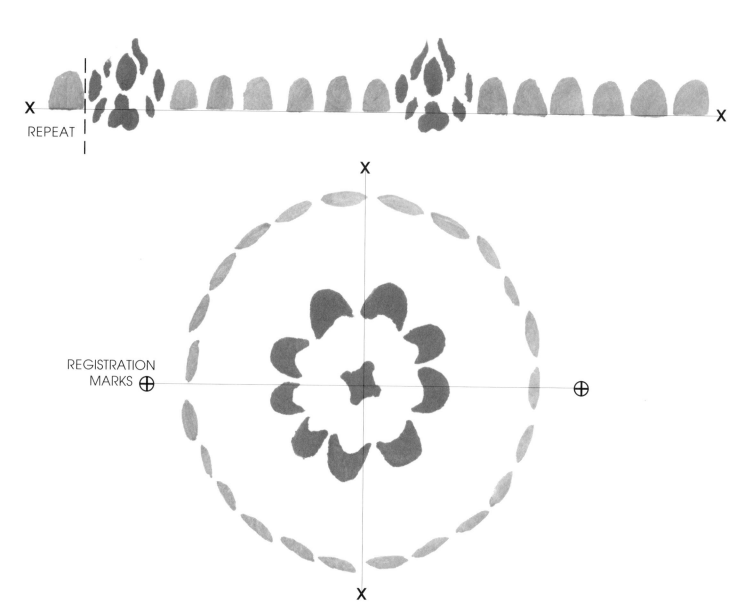

# NAPKIN RINGS

*(color page 91)*

**1**

Spray the leaf-and-stem stencil with adhesive or tape it to one of the napkin rings, and stencil the design. Once you have loaded your brush with paint, you will probably not need to add any more for the other rings.

**2**

Print the stencil for the cherries on each napkin ring.

**3**

When the paint is dry, give the napkin rings a coat of polyurethane. When dry, sand lightly with 000-grade steel wool. Apply another coat of polyurethane, and allow the rings to dry in a dust-free atmosphere.

## MATERIALS

Four 1-inch-wide (2.5 cm) wooden napkin rings

000-grade steel wool

One 9" x 12" (23 cm x 30 cm) stencil sheet and cutting tool

Stencil paint (2 colors)

Stencil brush

Paint tray

Scrap paper

Masking tape or adhesive stencil spray

½ pint (¾ litre) polyurethane, satin finish

REGISTRATION MARKS

ACTUAL SIZE

**TRACE AND CUT THE FOLLOWING STENCILS WITH 1½-INCH (4 CM) BORDERS:**

1. Leaves and stems

2. Cherries

*(color page 90)*

Apply a stencil design to one side of a bread board and leave the other side unfinished for the cutting surface.

## MATERIALS

A square or rectangular cutting board

150- and 220-grit sandpaper and tack cloth

Stencil sheet and cutting tool

3-inch-wide (7.5 cm) masking tape, gummed on one half

1-inch-wide (2.5 cm) masking tape

Ruler

Stencil paint (4 colors)

Paint tray

Scrap paper

Paint thinner and clean cloths

½ pint (¾ litre) polyurethane

Mineral oil

**1**

Sand the cutting board with first the 150-, then the 220-grit sandpaper; pick up the residue with a tack cloth.

**2**

To form a guide for a border stripe around the edge of the board, measure and with pencil draw a light line ½ inch (1.2 cm) from the edge all the way around. Place the 3-inch (7.5 cm) wide masking tape along the line, gummed side on the line, ungummed side facing in toward the center of the board. Place a strip of 1-inch (2.5 cm) wide masking tape ¼ inch (6 mm) outside the line. Take care at the corners to trim both tapes neatly so that the stripe will square properly. Paint within the lines of tape.

**3**

Find and mark the center of the board, side to side. Position the center mark of the leaf stencil over the center line. You may place the stencil at either the top or the bottom of the board. Stencil in the color, applying it most heavily on the outside tips of the leaves.

**4**

In a second color, stencil the birds and the peach.

**5**

In a third color, stencil the bird wings and beaks and the grapes.

**6**

In a fourth color, stencil the pear.

**7**

Coat the stencilled side of the cutting board with polyurethane, and allow it to dry. Be careful not to let the finish dribble down the sides of the bread board; only the stencilled surface should be coated. Follow the manufacturer's directions for additional coats, and sand between coats with the finest sandpaper. After the final coat dries, rub the unpainted side with mineral oil. (Mineral oil is the best sealant for wood surfaces that contact food; it is odorless, tasteless, colorless, and non-toxic.)

## TRACE AND CUT THE FOLLOWING STENCILS WITH 2-INCH (5 CM) BORDERS:

1. Leaves and stems

2. Birds (except wings and beaks) and peach

3. Bird beaks and wings, and grapes

4. Pear

REGISTRATION MARK

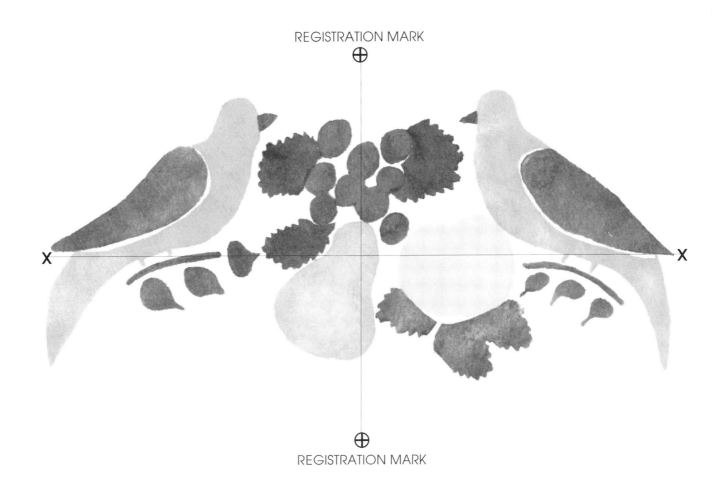

REGISTRATION MARK

ACTUAL SIZE

# FRAMED MIRROR

*(color page 95)*

I f your mirror frame has a wide header, use the design shown here, or choose one from another project in this book — the birds for the toaster cover, the flower sprigs for the fireplace wall border or the potholder, or the house for the dish cloth, all are good possibilities. Or, you may wish to create your own.

## MATERIALS

Mirror with a flat wooden frame

80-, 150-, and 220-grit sandpaper and tack cloth

½ pint (¾ litre) primer

½ pint (¾ litre) background paint

One 9" x 12" (23 cm x 30 cm) stencil sheet (you will need two sheets if your mirror has a header) and cutting tool

Stencil paint (2 colors)

Stencil brush

Paint tray

Scrap paper

Paint thinner and clean cloths

Masking tape or adhesive stencil spray

**1**
Prepare the wooden surface of the mirror by sanding with first 80-, then 150-, and last 220-grit sandpaper; always sand in the same direction as the wood grain. Vacuum up the residue, and pick up any dust with the tack cloth. Apply a coat of primer, and, when it is dry, sand lightly with 220-grit sandpaper. Apply two coats of background color, sanding lightly between coats.

**2**
Draw a light pencil line along the middle of each side to use as a guide to center the border on the frame.

**3**
Print the outer petals first. Spray the stencil with adhesive, or tape it in place while you are working. Print the circles and middle petals in the second color.

**4**
If your mirror has a header, center the design, and print first the pineapple leaves in the same color used for the outer petals, and then the pineapple with the second color.

## TRACE AND CUT THE FOLLOWING STENCILS WITH 2-INCH (5 CM) BORDERS:

1. Outer petals

2. Circles and middle petals

### For header (optional):

3. Pineapple leaves and outer petals

4. Pineapple, circles, and middle petals

REPEAT

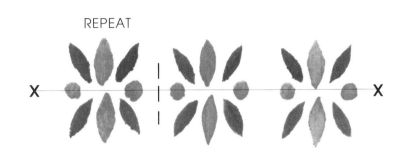

X                                    X

X

REGISTRATION
MARKS

⊕                                    ⊕

X

ACTUAL SIZE

# 5 STENCILLING WITH METALLIC POWDERS

As we have seen, colored stencils applied to chairs, tables, bureaus, and other furniture can be extremely effective. Another technique, popular since American colonial times, is to create a stencil design using metallic powders. Traditionally printed on a flat black or natural wood-grain surface, metallic powder stencils may also be printed over bright or rich colors.

Because the powders themselves are dry, they are applied through the stencil to an almost-dry coat of varnish to which they readily stick. Surface preparation is therefore particularly important. After sanding and before the first coat of paint or varnish, use a very fine grade of steel wool (0000) to smooth the surface to an even silkier sheen. Apply two coats of paint, sanding lightly between coats with the steel wool, and picking up residue first with a vacuum cleaner and then with a tack cloth. Lightly sand the second coat with the steel wool and make sure there is no dust on the chair. Any dust that gets into the varnish, which will be applied in the next step, will show when you apply the metallic powders. At this point, the finish should be very smooth to the touch.

With a very clean brush, apply a coat of varnish to the area to be stencilled, cover it with a dustcover (a clean box will do for this purpose), and allow it to dry until it is tacky — it should be sticky, but no varnish should come off on your finger when you touch it lightly.

To stencil, pour a small bit of powder onto a piece of paper and recap the bottle of powder. Wrap a 6-inch (15 cm) square of velvet around your finger so that there are no wrinkles or folds over the pad of your finger. (If you wish, you can sew a set of glovelike "fingers" for this purpose.) Put your stencil in place. In most cases, you will not need to tape it, as it is unlikely to

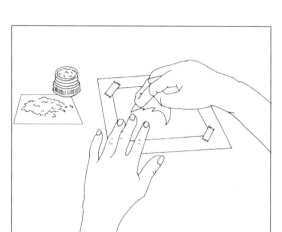

STENCILLING METALLIC POWDERS WITH A VELVET "FINGER."

slip on the sticky surface. Pick up a small amount of powder with your velvet-covered finger, tap any excess off on a piece of scrap paper (as with stencil paint, you need only a little), and pat the powder through the stencil. Metallic-powder stencils are often shaded, with more powder applied to the edges and less to the centers of rounded objects, and with little or no powder on parts of the design that should look as though they lie behind other parts. If you use different powders (bronze is the most common, but silver and gold are also available), use a separate piece of velvet for each powder.

Metallic powders are extremely fine and thus easily airborne. Pour out only a small amount at a time —a little goes a long way. You may wish to wear a mask to avoid inhaling the powder. Keep powders out of reach of young children.

When stencilling is complete, protect the design with a dustcover until the surface is thoroughly dry — at least 48 hours. Pick up any loose powder with a tack cloth and apply a final coat of varnish. Again protect it with a dustcover during the drying period. Give the piece a final, gentle rubbing with a fine-grade steel wool to remove any remaining bits of dust.

Depending on the humidity level, varnish usually remains tacky for about an hour. Prepare your stencils, powders, and velvet "fingers" ahead of time, so that you can begin to stencil as soon as the varnish is ready. Once the varnish begins to set up, you'll have to stop because the powder will no longer stick. Allow *at least* 24 hours for the varnish to dry completely. Carefully wash the surface with a damp cloth to remove excess powder, and then revarnish and continue as before.

To practice this technique, paint a piece of wood, cardboard, or even newspaper with two coats of flat, black, oil-based paint, allowing drying time between coats. Apply a coat of varnish, and allow it to dry as described above. As you stencil, experiment with how much powder to apply, what happens when you apply powder over powder, and how to shade figures on one side. Try building up a design, such as a bunch of grapes or a bouquet of flowers. After a bit of practice, you'll feel more confident when you approach the real thing.

The following four projects were designed specifically for the use of metallic powders, but you can use powders with many other stencils in this book. Small objects, such as boxes, are good beginners' projects. For example, fruits from the dining room wall border (pages 27-29) were used to decorate the painted boxes shown on page 90.

# CHAIR BACK

*(color page 91)*

The back horizontal slats of wooden chairs are obvious, and traditional, spots for a stencilled design. You may also wish to stencil a small design at the front of the seat to echo and accentuate the pattern on the back. This needn't be big or extensive — perhaps a little twig and flower. Stencilled stripes around the design or around the rungs can further set off the architectural features of the chair. You will find it easier to work if you lay the chair on its back to steady it. Curved backs may be particularly awkward.

## MATERIALS

6 chairs suitable for stencilling

150- and 220-grade sandpaper, 0000-grade steel wool, and tack cloth

1 pint (1 litre) flat, black paint

1 pint (1 litre) gloss varnish

Box to be used as a dustcover

Two 12" x 18" (30 cm x 45 cm) stencil sheets and cutting tool

Tape measure

Gold, silver, and green metallic powders

Three 6-inch (15 cm) squares of velvet fabric

Scrap paper

1 pint (1 litre) satin varnish

**1**

Prepare and paint the surface as described on page 85.

**2**

Apply a coat of varnish, and allow it to dry under a dustcover until it is ready for the stencil (see page 85).

**3**

Measure ½ inch (1.2 cm) down from the top of the chair back, and make a mark at the exact center.

**4**

With the gold powder, stencil the leaves. Position the leaf stencil so that the center mark on the stencil is on the mark made in Step 3. Be sure that the stencil is straight and tape it in place, if necessary (the tackiness of the varnish may hold the stencil securely enough that no tape is needed). Beginning with the outer leaves, pat around the outside of each leaf, leaving the center with little or no powder. Next, stencil the center leaf, again patting powder mostly around the outside of the leaf, but shading the center of this leaf a bit more darkly than those of the outer leaves. Stencil the small leaves and stems.

**5**

With another piece of velvet, pick up a little of the silver powder, and stencil the large flower blossoms on each side of the center leaf. Stencil the small flowers. If there is room, you may stencil additional small flowers, here and there as you wish.

**6**

Change applicators and use green powder to stencil the veins for the outside and center leaves; taper off the color as you get near the larger flowers.

**7**

Allow the chair to continue drying for at least forty-eight hours. When it is completely dry, pick up any loose powder with a tack cloth, apply a coat of satin finish, and protect the chair with a dustcover while it is drying. Give the chair a final rubbing with very fine-grade steel wool to remove any remaining bits of dust.

X

1 SQUARE = 1 INCH

REGISTRATION
MARKS

X

**TRACE AND CUT THE
FOLLOWING STENCILS WITH
A 1½-INCH (4 CM) BORDER:**

1. Leaves

2. Flowers

3. Leaf veins

◀ STENCILLED BORDER ON GARDEN TABLE TAKEN FROM "CURTAINS," PAGES 144-45.

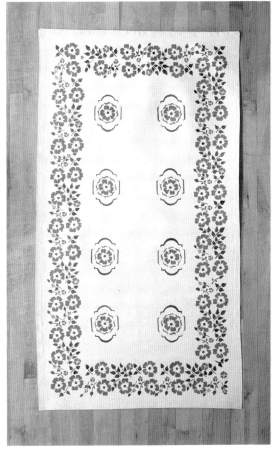

▲ FLOOR CLOTH, PAGES 52-54.

◀ STENCILLED BORDER ON LAMP SHADE TAKEN FROM "CEILING BORDER AND WALL PANEL," PAGES 20-23.

▲ DISH TOWELS, PAGES 120-21.

▲ CUTTING BOARD, PAGES 80-81.

▼ TOTE BAG WITH CATTAILS, PAGES 112-13.

▲ STENCILLED FRUIT ON WOODEN BOXES TAKEN FROM "FRUIT BORDER AND STRIPES FOR A DINING ROOM," PAGES 27-29.

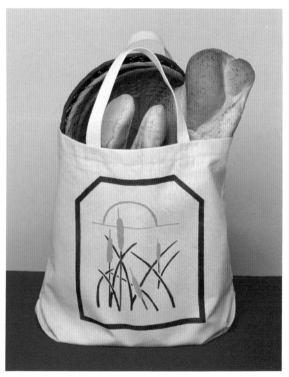

▲  QUILTED HOT PADS, PAGES 138-39.

▶  QUILTED PLACEMATS AND NAPKINS,
PAGES 136-37.

▲  CHAIR BACK, PAGES 87-88.

▼  NAPKIN RINGS, PAGE 79.

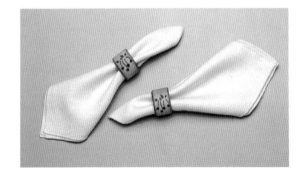

▲  BAKER'S APRON, PAGES 116-17.

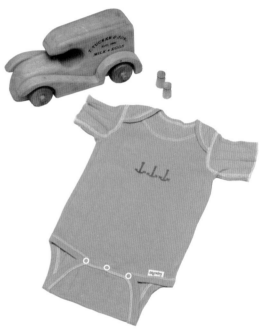

▲  LAYETTE SET, PAGES 106-7.

▼  SWEATSHIRT, PAGES 108-9.

▲  ONE-PIECE SUIT, FROM "LAYETTE SET,"
   PAGES 106-7.

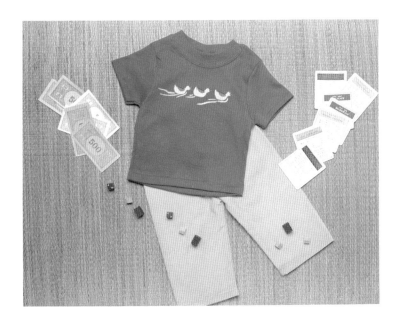

◄  TEE SHIRT, FROM PAGE 105.

▲  STENCILLED HEARTS ON BABY SHOES FROM "DOLL'S CHAIR," PAGES 68-69.

▲  STENCILLED ROCKING HORSE ON ONE-PIECE SUIT FROM "DOLL'S CHAIR," PAGES 68-69.

▶  DOLL'S CHAIR, PAGES 68-69.

▲   PENNSYLVANIA DUTCH-STYLE HOPE
CHEST, PAGES 59-62.

▲   WOODEN BOX, PAGES 76-78.

▼   QUILTED PILLOWS, PAGES 133-35.

▲   PILLOWCASE AND SHEET SET, PAGES
124-25.

▲ STENCIL DESIGNS ON WOODEN BOX FROM "BUREAU," PAGES 56-58.

▲ KNITTING BAG, PAGES 114-15.

▲ DETAIL, STENCILLED QUILT, PAGES 126-32.

▲ MIRROR, PAGES 82-83.

◀ STENCIL PATTERNS ON CARDS AND GIFTWRAP MAY BE FOUND ON PAGES 70, 68, 116, 118, 124, 133, AND 151.

▲ LAMP BASE, PAGES 142-43, STATIONARY, PAGES 152-53.

▲ WASTEBASKET, PAGES 74-75; EMBROIDERED GUEST TOWELS, PAGES 122-23.

# BOSTON-STYLE ROCKER

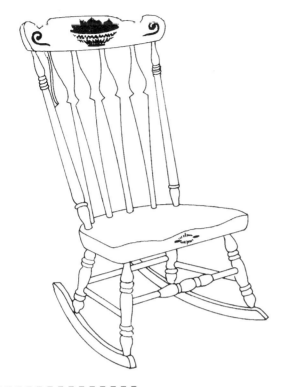

**1**

Prepare the chair as suggested on page 85. Apply a coat of primer and two coats of the background paint, sanding and picking up all dust with a vacuum cleaner and tack cloth between each coat.

**2**

Apply a coat of varnish, and allow it to dry under a dustcover until it is ready for the stencil (see page 85).

**3**

With gold powder, stencil the compote centered on the chair back. Also with gold, stencil in the scrollwork at the ends of the slat.

**4**

Stencil the peach above the compote rim; pat on the powder heavily at the top and fade to nothing at the rim to give it an appearance of sitting inside the rim. Stencil mostly in gold, but highlight the shape a bit with bronze for a rounded effect. Use bronze to stencil the cleft in the peach. In the same manner, stencil the melon and the pear. Use bronze powder to stencil the melon segments. Stencil the grapes in bronze powder.

**5**

Stencil the leaves, shading more heavily on the outside tips and tapering to nothing where they go behind the fruit.

**6**

Use silver for the wheat. Taper the stems to nothing as they fit behind the fruit.

**7**

Center the design for the front of the seat, and stencil it with gold powder.

**8**

Protect the chair with the dustcover, and allow the varnish to finish drying. When the varnish is completely dry (about forty-eight hours), wipe off any excess powder so it won't smear when the final coats of varnish are applied. Apply two protective coats of varnish, polishing gently with very fine-grade steel wool between coats, and remove any dust particles. Let the chair dry under the dustcover.

**TRACE AND CUT THE FOLLOWING STENCILS WITH 1½-INCH (4 CM) BORDERS:**

1. Compote
2. Melon
3. Melon segments
4. Pear
5. Peach
6. Peach cleft
7. Wheat (Prick the stencil material with a pin to make the wheat heads)
8. Grapes
9. Leaves
10. Design for the seat front
11. Scrollwork for the top slat ends

REGISTRATION MARK ⊕

REGISTRATION MARK ⊕

ACTUAL SIZE

# ····· END TABLE WITH DRAWER ··············

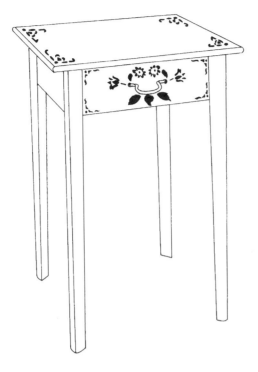

The floral design is meant to frame the drawer pull. You may have to adjust the arrangement slightly to fit around the pull.

## MATERIALS

End table with drawer

80-, 150-, and 220-grit sandpaper, 0000-grade steel wool, and tack cloth

½ pint (¾ litre) primer

½ pint (¾ litre) background paint

½ (¾ litre) pint varnish

Box to be used as a dustcover

Three 12" x 18" (30 cm x 45 cm) stencil sheets and cutting tool

Gold, bronze, and silver metallic powders

Three 6-inch (15 cm) squares of velvet fabric

½ pint (¾ litre) polyurethane

**1**
Remove the drawer hardware, and prime and paint the surface of the table for stencilling as suggested on page 85.

**2**
Apply a coat of varnish to the top and drawer, and allow it to dry under the dustcover until it is ready for the stencil (see page 85). If you want a stripe of gold around the legs, apply varnish there also.

**3**
Remove the drawer and stand it on end so that you can stencil on a horizontal surface. With gold powder, print a corner design in each corner of the top surface and drawer. Use whichever size design is most in scale with the table. The smaller design may be better for the drawer corners, while the larger design may work well for the top. Stencil these designs fairly evenly, with no shading.

**4**
If you are stencilling a band of gold around the legs, wrap a straight edge of stencil sheet around the leg so that it marks one side of a band; stencil about half the width of the band. Move the sheet to the top edge and complete the band.

**5**
On the drawer, stencil the tulip with bronze powder, shading it more heavily on its outside points than at its center.

**6**
Use a third piece of velvet to stencil the daisies with silver, shading fairly evenly over the surface of the blossoms.

**7**
Stencil the leaves with gold powder; print the tips of the leaves heavily, shading to nothing at the base.

**8**

Allow the varnish to finish drying (about forty-eight hours), and then wipe off any excess powder. Apply a coat or two of polyurethane over the varnish to make a waterproof finish (particularly important on the top of the table). Satin-finish polyurethane looks better for a final coat; stir it after each brushful so it doesn't streak.

REGISTRATION MARKS

X

X

1 SQUARE = 1 INCH

**TRACE AND CUT THE FOLLOWING STENCILS WITH 1½-INCH (4 CM) BORDERS:**

1. Small corner design

2. Large corner design

3. Tulips

4. Leaves

5. Daisies

# FIREPLACE BELLOWS

## MATERIALS

Wooden bellows

150- and 220-grit sandpaper and tack cloth

½ pint (¾ litre) background paint (optional)

Varnish

Box to be used as a dustcover

Two 12" x 18" (30 cm x 45 cm) stencil sheets and cutting tool

Gold and bronze metallic powders

Two 6-inch (15 cm) pieces of velvet fabric

Pumice and lemon oil

**1**
Sand the bellows lightly with 150- and then 220-grit sandpaper. Wipe off the residue with a tack cloth, and apply two coats of background color paint; between coats sand with 220-grit sandpaper and pick up the residue with a tack cloth.

**2**
Apply a coat of varnish, and allow it to dry until it is ready for stencilling (see page 85). Place a dustcover over the bellows while the varnish is drying.

**3**
Find the center bottom of the bellows, measure up 1 inch (2.5 cm), and make a mark to position the base of the compote. Using gold metallic powder, stencil the compote; shade it evenly over the entire shape.

**4**
With gold powder, stencil the leaves to the right and left of the compote rim. Also with gold powder, stencil the melon.

**5**
With bronze powder, stencil the fruits. Apply more color at the top of each fruit and fade into nothing as it disappears behind the rim of the compote or another fruit.

**6**
Use gold powder for the leaves above the fruit. Make them much darker at the outside tips than at their centers and bottoms. Stencil the veins at the center of each leaf.

**7**
Allow the varnish to dry completely (at least 24 hours). Wipe any excess powder off the bellows with the tack cloth. Apply a coat of varnish over the stencilling, and let it dry under a dustcover. Sand lightly with 220-grit sandpaper, being careful not to damage the stencilling. Again, wipe with a tack cloth. Apply the final coat of varnish, and allow it to dry under a dustcover. For a beautiful finish, rub with pumice and lemon oil.

**TRACE AND CUT THE
FOLLOWING STENCILS WITH
2-INCH (5 CM) BORDERS:**

1. Compote

2. Leaves

3. Leaf veins

4. Fruits

REGISTRATION MARK

ACTUAL SIZE

REGISTRATION MARK

# 6 STENCILLING ON FABRIC

Stencilling on fabric is as easy as stencilling on wood or walls. Unique gifts can be made by applying a stencil design to baby's bib or tee shirt or to a child's sweatshirt. Curtains, placemat and napkin sets, throw pillows, and even quilts can be stencilled.

Fabric paint is usually available in art or craft stores, as well as many large fabric stores. Look for paint that is colorfast, washable, and dry cleanable. Some fabric paints need to be thinned with a special medium so that they will flow over the fabric properly; follow the manufacturer's instructions. You can also use screen-printing ink designed for fabric; it can be applied with a stencil brush, comes in many colors (which can be mixed together to make other colors), and is water-soluble, making clean up easy. Artist-brand acrylic paints (in tubes) have a nice consistency, and they, too, are water-soluble; they may, however, make the fabric a bit stiff. You will also find solid, oil-based paints in stick form and fabric-painting dyes in squeeze bottles. Experiment to determine which works best for you and for your project. Recent years have seen an explosion of interest in painting on fabric, and the variety of materials and supplies has increased proportionately; check in your favorite store for new products.

Cut the stencil from the same kind of materials used for walls or furniture (see page 2). Or, if you are stencilling only one or a few motifs, adhesive papers make very good stencils for use on fabric. The paper is easy to cut, stays firmly in place while you work, and pulls up readily when you are through.

Before stencilling, launder the fabric to remove factory sizing and to preshrink the piece. Iron the fabric, if necessary. If you have to mark the fabric to help you position the stencil, use a washable marker or a "disappearing" marker, available in fabric stores, or make *very light* marks with pencil or chalk. If you use washable marker, be sure to wash your piece thoroughly after stencilling to remove marks or they may reappear. Do not iron over the marks before washing or they may leave a brown mark; this may be awkward to avoid if you must iron the design to set it (see below), so keep this in mind when you are planning your work. Before you mark the fabric extensively, test a scrap to make sure that guide marks really can be completely removed.

When you are ready to stencil, tape or clip your fabric to a smooth, hard surface protected by a piece of plastic or foil; because fabric is porous, paint may seep through it to the surface below. Tape your stencil in place, or use adhesive spray to anchor it. Because the fabric may give a bit as you brush or scrub paint into it, you must make everything as stable as possible to avoid blurring the design. If you are printing a tubular piece, such as a pillowcase or a tee shirt, tuck a padding of newspapers or a magazine topped with a plain piece of paper between the layers of fabric to keep the bottom layer clean.

As with other stencils, use very little paint on your brush, and apply it with a dabbing motion. Build up the color gradually and avoid too-thick layers of paint, which can make the fabric stiff. Let the weave of the fabric show through the paint.

When stencilling light-colored paint on dark fabrics, apply a coat of white through the stencil first, allow it to dry, and then apply the color you wish. Do not remove the stencil between coats as it is extremely difficult, if not impossible, to line up the stencil accurately for subsequent printings.

Fabric paints must usually be permanently "set" by ironing them for a few minutes with a hot iron. Follow the instructions included with the paint you use. This is an important step, for if not set, the stencilling may wash off.

# CHILD'S TEE SHIRT

*(color page 93)*

**1**

Position the stencil of the water and ducks so that it is centered on the front of the shirt, with the bottom of the water level with the bottom of the armholes. Tape the stencil in place and print it.

**2**

Stencil the eyes, beaks, and wings with the second color.

**3**

To set the design, follow the directions that are included with the paint you use.

## MATERIALS

Plain tee shirt, any light solid color

One 9" x 12" (23 cm x 30 cm) stencil sheet and cutting tool

Tape measure

Fabric paint (2 colors)

Stencil brush

Paint tray

Scrap paper

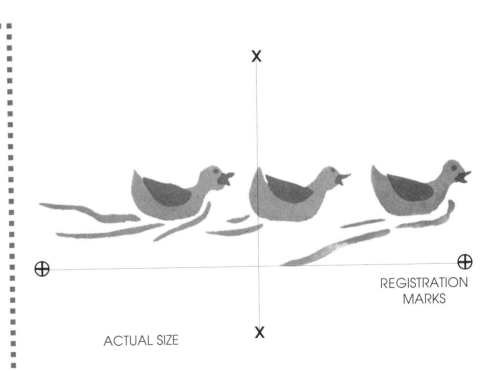

**REGISTRATION MARKS**

ACTUAL SIZE

**TRACE AND CUT THE FOLLOWING STENCILS WITH 2-INCH (5 CM) BORDERS:**

1. Water and ducks

2. Wings, eyes, and beaks

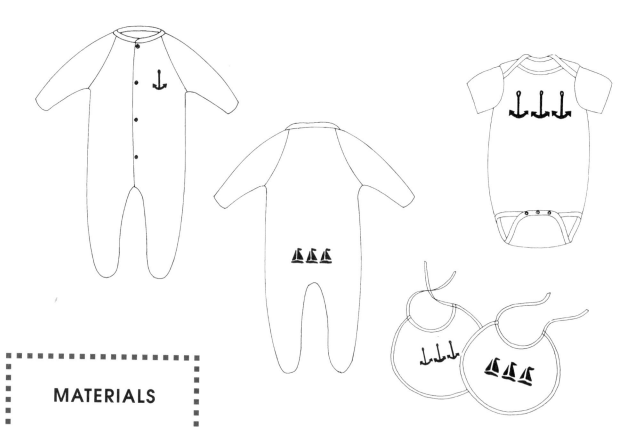

## MATERIALS

2 white or light-colored
baby bibs

2 white or light-colored
one-piece stretch suits

1 white or light-colored
undershirt

One 9" x 12" (23 cm x 30
cm) stencil sheet and
cutting tool

Tape measure

Fabric paint (2 colors)

Stencil brush

Paint tray

Scrap paper

**1**

Tape one of the bibs to a firm surface. Make light marks at the exact center and 1 inch (2.5 cm) on either side of the center mark. Position the boat stencil so that the center bottom of the middle boat is on the center mark and the other boats are on the other marks. Tape the stencil in place, and print the design. Print the sails in a second color. Print the sailboats and flags on the back of the stretch suits about 1 inch (2.5 cm) below waist level.

**2**

On the second bib, mark the center, as well as 1 inch (1.9 cm) on either side of the center. Print a row of anchors along these marks. For more color, use two or three different colors for the anchors. Print a row of anchors at the center front of the undershirt, about 2½ inches (6.5 cm) down from the neckline. Print one anchor on the left front of each stretch suit; block the other anchors on the stencil with masking tape, so that you don't accidentally print them.

**3**

To set the design, follow the directions that are included with the paint you use.

## TRACE AND CUT THE FOLLOWING STENCILS WITH 2-INCH (5 CM) BORDERS:

1. Boats and flags

2. Sails

3. Anchors

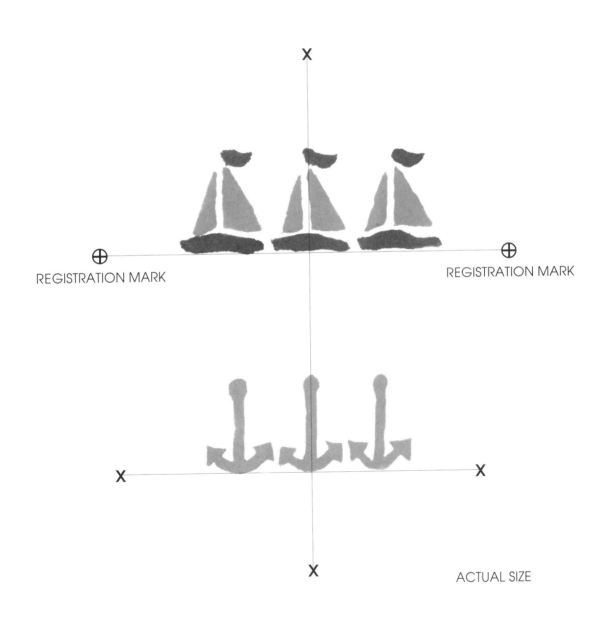

X

REGISTRATION MARK

REGISTRATION MARK

X         X

X

ACTUAL SIZE

What child wouldn't enjoy a cozy sweatshirt, printed with his or her own name and a favorite activity. Use the train riding the oval track that is pictured here, or create your own design of balloons, flowers, airplanes, or sports motifs. Make this design in your child's favorite colors, bright or pastel.

## MATERIALS

Plain-colored sweatshirt

Lettering stencils (available in art-supply stores)

Washable fabric marker

One 9" x 12" (23 x 30 cm) and one 12" x 18" (30 cm x 45 cm) stencil sheet and cutting tool

Tape measure

Fabric paint

Stencil brush

Scrap paper

**1**
With washable fabric marker, draw a line across the front of the sweatshirt from the bottom of one of the armholes to the other. Lay the stencil design on the shirt with the track centered over the line to make sure there is room for the entire design; for small sizes you may have to print the design somewhat lower. Place the center letter (or letters) of the child's name at the middle of the sweatshirt, and arrange the other letters around it, taking care to space them accurately. Be sure to place them closely enough together that there is room for the track to be stenciled around the name. Tape each of the letters to the line, and print them. Several letters can be stenciled with one brushload of paint; try to keep the shade even throughout so that no letter is darker or lighter than the letters next to it.

**2**
Stencil the oval track around the name.

**3**
Stencil the coal car to the left of the center at the top of the oval, with the wheels just a bit higher than the track. Stencil this car again, upside down, at the bottom of the track (again with the wheels just off the track).

**4**
Print the engine in front of the coal car, top and bottom. Print the box cars and then the cabooses behind the coal cars.

**5**
Print the engine smoke above the smokestack and running back over the top of the engine top and bottom.

**6**
To set the design, follow the directions included with the paint.

**TRACE AND CUT THE FOLLOWING STENCILS WITH 2-INCH (5 CM) BORDERS:**

1. Oval track

2. Engine

3-5. One stencil for each car

6. Wheels (optional: cut these on a separate stencil only if you wish to print them in a color other than the car colors)

7. Smoke

8. For stencil alphabet, see page 157

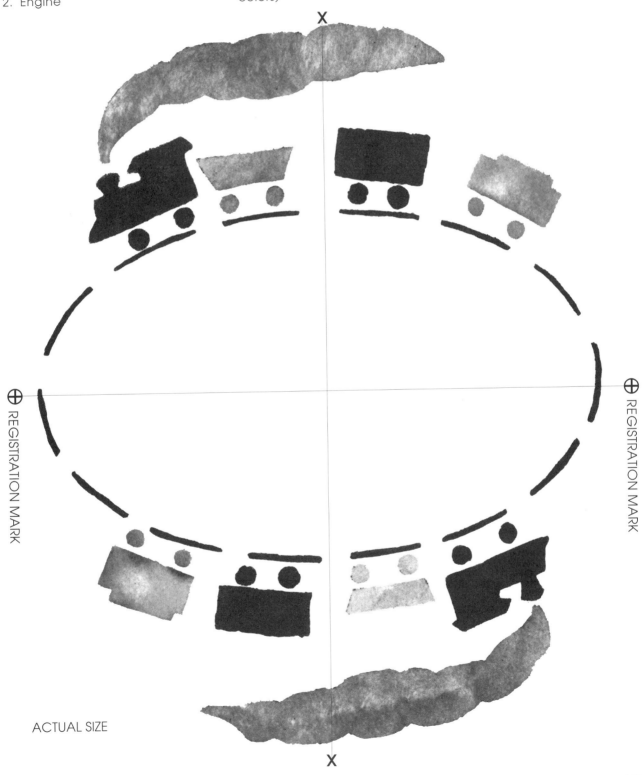

ACTUAL SIZE

# TOTE BAG WITH
# STENCILLED LANDSCAPE

Canvas tote bags may be bought in many styles, some absolutely plain, and some with colored fabric handles and center panels. You can also make your own from a heavy muslin with a purchased pattern.

## MATERIALS

A tote bag (white or off-white)

Tape measure

Three 9" x 12" (23 x 30 cm) stencil sheets and cutting tool

Stencil paint (3 colors)

Stencil brush

Paint tray

Paint thinner and clean cloths

Scrap paper

**1**
Measure the width of your tote bag and enlarge the stencil pattern to equal the width of the bag.

**2**
Tape the mountain stencil to the tote, centered top to bottom and with the sides of the stencil design even with the sides of the bag. Print it on both sides of the bag.

**3**
Stencil the island in a second color (use the registration marks to position the design accurately).

**4**
Stencil the barn and house in a third color.

**5**
To set the design, follow the instructions that are included with the paint you use.

**TRACE AND CUT THE
FOLLOWING STENCILS WITH
2-INCH (5 CM) BORDERS:**

1. Mountains

2. Island

3. Barn and house

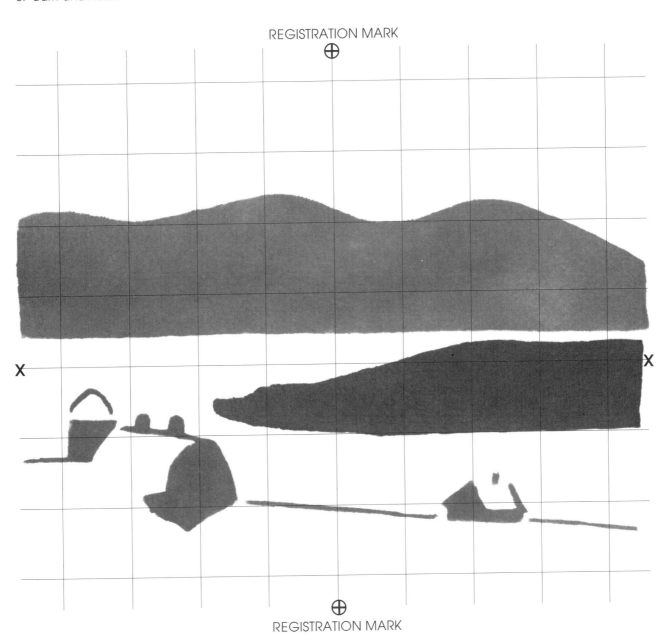

REGISTRATION MARK
⊕

X                                                                    X

⊕
REGISTRATION MARK

# TOTE BAG WITH STENCILLED CATTAILS

*(color page 90)*

The supply list for this project is the same as that for the Tote Bag with Stencilled Landscape. This design requires only two 9" x 12" (23 x 30 cm) stencil sheets and two colors, however, one for the frame and cattails, and one for the rushes.

## MATERIALS

A tote bag (white or off-white)

Tape measure

3-inch-wide (7.5 cm) masking tape, gummed on one half

Three 9" x 12" (23 x 30 cm) stencil sheets and cutting tool

Stencil paint (2 colors)

Stencil brush

Paint tray

Paint thinner and clean cloths

Scrap paper

**1**
Measure to find the centers of both sides of the tote. Measure out from the center to create a rectangle, 10" wide x 14" tall (25 cm wide x 35 cm tall). (This can be made larger or smaller, depending on the size of the tote.) Make marks 2 inches (5 cm) away from each corner on all four sides of the rectangle. Draw lines connecting these marks to cut off the corners. Erase the lines forming the original corners.

**2**
Place tape along the pencilled lines, gummed edge on the line, ungummed side toward the outside of the tote. When you come to a corner, tear the tape, and begin laying tape on the next line. Place a second line of tape ½ inch (1.2 cm) inside the first, this time with the ungummed side facing the center of the tote. Stencil the stripe within the lines. Repeat on the other side of the bag.

**3**
Position the stencil of the stems and leaves so that it is centered within the frame, and print it on both sides of the bag.

**4**
Position the stencil for the flower spikes over the stems, and print.

**5**
To set the design, follow the instructions that are included with the paint you use.

**TRACE AND CUT THE FOLLOWING STENCILS WITH 2-INCH (5 CM) BORDERS:**

1. Stems and leaves

2. Flower spikes, sun, and water

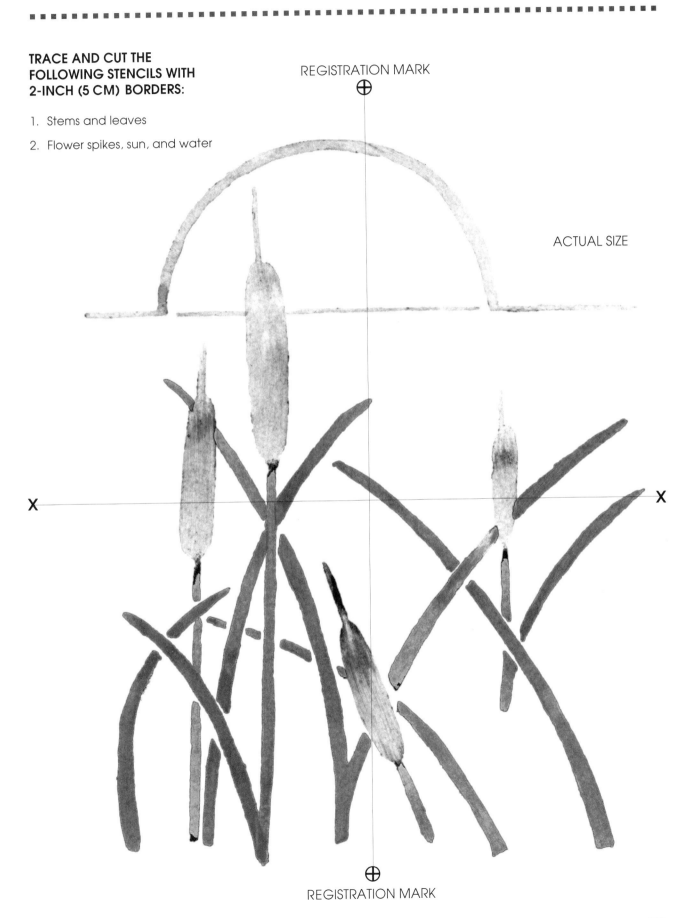

REGISTRATION MARK
⊕

ACTUAL SIZE

X ——————————————————————————————— X

⊕
REGISTRATION MARK

### MATERIALS

1½ yards (1.5 m) unbleached or plain-colored fabric and thread to match

1½ yards (1.5 m) contrasting calico print fabric

Tape measure

Two 12" x 18" (30 cm x 45 cm) stencil sheets and cutting tool

Fabric paint (3 colors)

Stencil brush

Paint tray

Scrap paper

Two 2½-yard (2.3 m) pieces of cord, suitable for a drawstring

Single-fold bias tape (or make bias strips to match either plain or calico fabric)

**1**

Cut one 15-inch (38 cm) diameter circle from the plain-colored fabric and another from the calico. Cut one 15" x 50" (38 cm x 1.35 m) rectangle from each kind of fabric.

**2**

Make a mark at the center of the plain-colored fabric piece, 8 inches up from the bottom. Center the stencil for the leaves on the mark, and print.

**3**

With the second and third colors, stencil the flowers, again using the center marks for positioning.

**4**

To set the design, follow the instructions that are included with the paint you use.

**5**

For the lining, fold the 15" x 50" (38 cm x 1.35 m) piece of calico in half crosswise, with right sides together. Stitch the 15-inch (38 cm) ends in a ⅝-inch (1.6 cm) seam. Stitch this tube to the calico circular bottom, right sides together. Fold the bag in half lengthwise and make marks 2 inches (5 cm) from the top on each side for buttonholes for the drawstrings to come through. Sew and cut the buttonholes.

**6**

For the bag, sew the plain-colored fabric pieces in the same way you sewed the calico in Step 2, but do not make buttonholes this time.

**7**

Put the calico bag inside the plain-colored bag, wrong sides facing. Stitch 2¼ inches (6 cm) below the outside edge to form one seam for the drawstring; make a second line of stitching 1 inch (2.5 cm) above the first one. Bind off the raw edges with bias tape (see page 128).

**8**

Feed the drawstrings into the seam, threading each one all the way around the bag, with both ends of one string coming through the buttonhole on one side, and both ends of the other string coming through the other buttonhole. Tie a knot in the ends of both pairs of strings.

**TRACE AND CUT THE FOLLOWING STENCILS WITH 2-INCH (5 CM) BORDERS:**

1. Leaves and stems
2. Three large flowers
3. Remaining flowers

⊕ REGISTRATION MARK

X ⸻ X

1 SQUARE = 1 INCH

REGISTRATION MARK ⊕

# BAKER'S APRON

*(color page 91)*

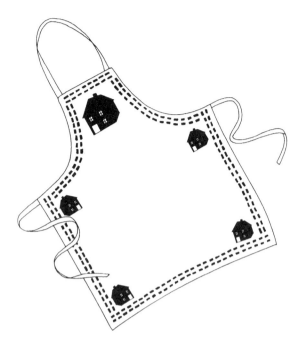

This apron has five stencilled houses: one centered on the bib 3 inches (7.5 cm) down from the top; one on each side, 3 inches (7.5 cm) in from the point where the ties are attached; and one on each side at the bottom corners, 3 inches (7.5 cm) up from the bottom and 3 inches (7.5 cm) in from the sides. Use a dark color (even black) for the windows and doors, as they are printed on top of the house color. Note that the pattern was enlarged and a second stencil cut for the house centered on the bib.

## MATERIALS

A baker's apron with bib and tie strings

One 9" x 12" (23 cm x 30 cm) and two 12" x 18" (30 cm x 45 cm) stencil sheets and cutting tool

Fabric paint (3 colors)

Stencil brush

Paint tray

Scrap paper

Tape measure

Masking tape

**1**

Stencil the solid background of each house, positioned as described in introduction. Use the center marks on the stencil to place the design on the straight of the fabric. Make light pencil marks to help you line up stencils 2 and 3. Reverse the stencil to print the designs on the left side of the apron, so that all houses face into the center.

**2**

With the same color, stencil the border, 1 inch (2.5 cm) from the edge all around. Tape the stencil as you print. Stencil across the top and bottom of the bib first (follow suggestions on pages 15-16 for printing continuous borders). Next, beginning at the bottom left corner of the apron above the horizontal border, stencil the border up the left side until you reach the border at the top of the bib; do not overlap any prints. Stencil the right border from bottom to top to match the left border.

**3**

With the second color, print the roofs and chimneys; use the center marks for positioning.

**4**

With the third color, print the door and window panes.

**5**

To set the paint, follow the instructions that are included with the paint you use.

**TRACE AND CUT THE
FOLLOWING STENCILS WITH
2-INCH (5 CM) BORDERS:**

1. House

2. Roof and chimney

3. Windows and door

4. Double broken line (border)

ACTUAL SIZE

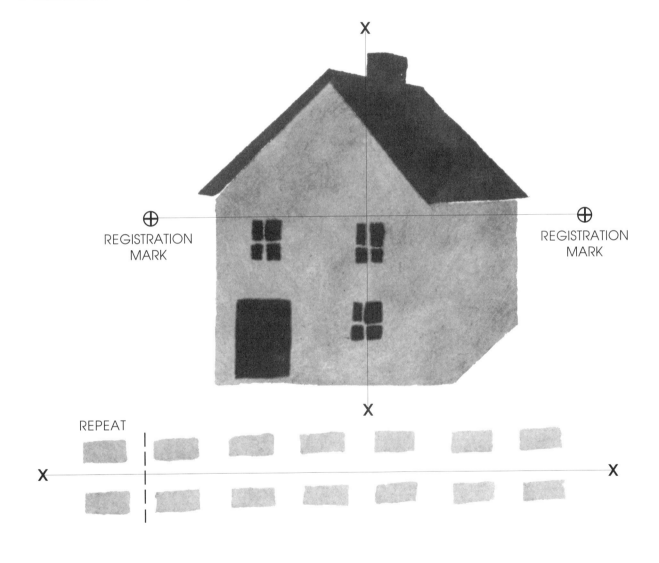

REGISTRATION
MARK

REGISTRATION
MARK

REPEAT

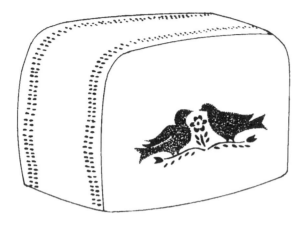

These directions are for a toaster cover, but they can be adapted to use for any appliance.

## MATERIALS

½ yard (45 cm) unbleached muslin or other plain fabric and thread to match

Two 12" x 18" (30 cm x 45 cm) stencil sheets and cutting tool

Masking tape

Fabric paint (3 colors)

Stencil brush

Paint tray

Tape measure

Scrap paper

**1**

Measure and cut the fabric pieces as follows: (A) For the length of the center strip, measure from the bottom of one end of the toaster, across the top, and down to the bottom of the other end, and add 2 inches (5 cm); for the width, measure across the top of the toaster, and add 2 inches (5 cm); cut one rectangle of this size. (B) For the side panels, measure length and width and add 2 inches (5 cm) to each measurement; cut two pieces to these dimensions.

**2**

On the center strip, stencil the border along both long edges, placing the design about 1½ inches (4 cm) away from the raw edge. Follow the suggestions on pages 15-16 for stencilling continuous borders.

**3**

Make a light mark at the center of both side panels; draw a guide line out from the center in both directions, parallel to the top edge. Position the bird and flower stencil with the center of the flower on the center mark, and the registration marks on the guide line. Print this stencil on both side panels with the same color as used for the borders. Allow this print to dry thoroughly before proceeding.

**4**

With the second color, print the birds' wings and the remaining flowers.

**5**

With the third color, print the leaves and stems.

**6**

With right sides together, pin the center strip to the sides and top of the stencilled panels. Stitch, taking ⅝-inch (1.4 cm) seams. Lift the presser foot and pivot on the needle to turn the corners. Clip the seam to the corners on the center strip. Hem the bottom edge, turning under 1 inch (2.5 cm).

**7**

To set the design, follow the directions that come with the paint you use.

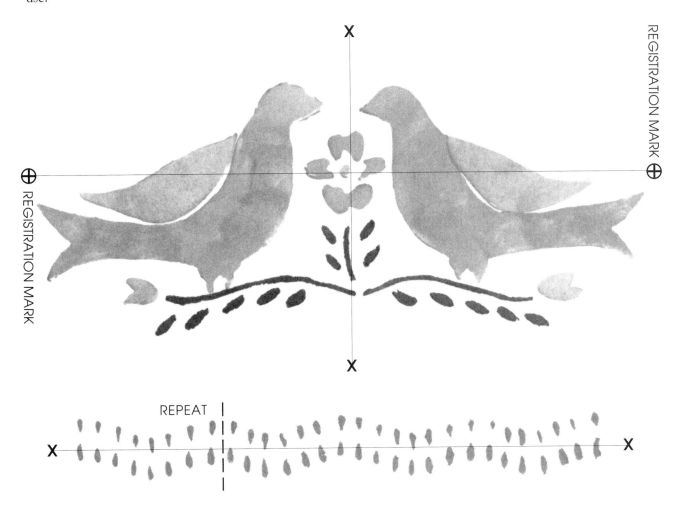

ACTUAL SIZE

**TRACE AND CUT THE FOLLOWING STENCILS WITH 2-INCH (5 CM) BORDERS:**

1. Border

2. Bird bodies and center flower petals

3. Bird wings, flower center, and tulips

4. Leaves and stems

*(color page 90)*

Stencilled dish towels are an ideal handmade, yet inexpensive, gift—always useful as well as attractive. Be sure to use a highly absorbent fabric, such as linen or 100 percent cotton.

## MATERIALS

1yard (1 m) of 36-inch (1 m) wide fabric and thread to match

Tape measure

Two 12" x 18" (30 cm x 45 cm) stencil sheets and cutting tool

Fabric paint (4 colors, 1 very dark for the windows)

Stencil brush

Paint tray

Scrap paper

**1**

Cut two towels, each 18" x 30" (45 cm x 75 cm). Make a narrow hem on all sides.

**2**

Print the border design 1½ inches (4 cm) from the edge, first along the bottom, then along the top, and last along the sides. Tape the stencil in place when you print. Follow the suggestions on pages 15-16 for printing continuous borders. On the sides, stencil the border between the top and bottom borders and be careful not to paint over prints already made.

**3**

Make a light mark at the exact center of the towel, 3 inches (7.5 cm) above the bottom border. Tape the house stencil to the towel, with the door centered over the mark. In the same color used for the border, stencil in the house and chimneys.

**4**

Position the roof and fence stencil so that the bottom of the fence is slightly higher than the bottom of the house. In the second color, print the fence and roof.

**5**

Place the willow stencil so the base of the trunk is even with the bottom of the fence. Print the third color.

**6**

When the house color is thoroughly dry, print the windows.

**7**

To set the design, follow the instructions included with the paint you use.

**TRACE AND CUT THE FOLLOWING STENCILS WITH 2-INCH (5 CM) BORDERS:**

1. Border
2. House and chimneys
3. Roof and fences
4. Willows and front yard
5. Windows

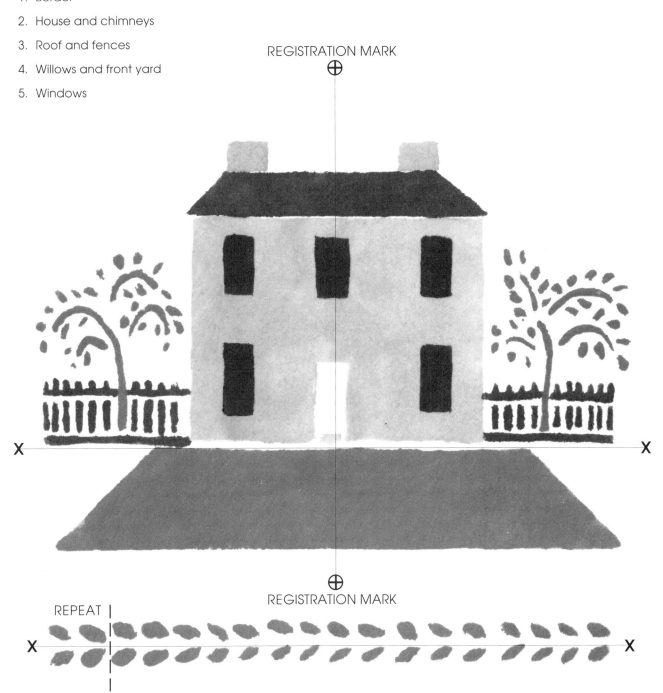

REGISTRATION MARK

REGISTRATION MARK

X — X

REPEAT

X — X

ACTUAL SIZE

# STENCILLED AND EMBROIDERED GUEST TOWELS

*(color page 96)*

M any craft stores carry terry cloth fingertip towels with a plain-weave band across the bottom. The plain-weave band provides a good surface for stencilling and/or embroidery. In this project, the stencilled flowers are highlighted by an outline of stem stitch done in matching embroidery floss.

## MATERIALS

A set of four guest towels, in plain, light colors

Tape measure

3-inch-wide (7.5 cm) masking tape, gummed on one half

Five 9" x 12" (23 cm x 30 cm) stencil sheets and cutting tool

Fabric paint (3 colors— green for the leaves and stems, and 2 other colors for the buds and flowers)

Stencil brush

Paint tray

Scrap paper

Embroidery floss (3 colors, to match the stencil paint)

**1**

Spread a towel out in front of you with the bottom hem toward you. If the towel has a band, mark it at the exact center. Otherwise, make a mark 3 inches (7.5 cm) up from the bottom at the center of the towel.

**2**

Position the stencil for the stem and leaves so that the top of the stem is on the center mark. Tape it down, and stencil in the design. Repeat on each of the other guest towels.

**3**

Print each towel with a different flower design — half the towels in one color, and half in another. Use the registration marks to position the prints accurately.

**4**

To set the designs, follow the instructions included with the paint you use.

**5**

Thread a needle with three strands of the green embroidery floss for the leaves and stem. Make a knot at the end. Bring the needle up from the back at the base of the

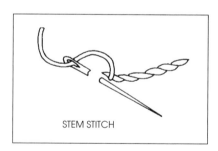

STEM STITCH

stem, and make a line of stem stitching along the stem and leaves to outline the stencilled shapes. (To stem stitch, take a stitch about ¼ inch (6 mm) long. Start the next stitch about three-quarters of the way along the first stitch. Proceed in this manner, to form a continuous line.)

**6**

As in Step 5, outline the flowers

and buds, with thread to match each flower. Don't carry the thread from the bud to the flower in one long stitch; tie off and begin again.

REGISTRATION MARKS ⊕

X ————————————— X

**TRACE AND CUT THE FOLLOWING STENCILS WITH 2-INCH (5 CM) BORDERS:**

1.   Leaves and stems

2–5. One stencil for each flower and the bud

ACTUAL SIZE

# PILLOWCASE AND SHEET SET

*(color page 94)*

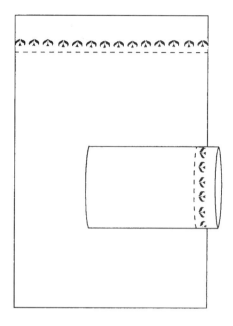

$A$ small, two-color running border along the hem, or just above it gives the same effect as embroidery — and can be done in much less time.

## MATERIALS

1 set pillowcases, white or a plain color

1 top sheet, white or a plain color

One 9" x 12" (23 x 30 cm) stencil sheet and cutting tool

Fabric paint (2 colors)

Stencil brush

Paint tray

Scrap paper

**1**

Place one end of the top of the sheet on a firm surface, and tape it down. Position the first border stencil with the design just inside the hemline. Be sure to position it so that the design will be right side up when you turn down the sheet on the bed (see illustration above). Print across the entire hem, following the suggestions on pages 15-16 for printing continuous borders.

**2**

Stencil the same border on the pillowcases, starting at the side seam and going all the way around the hem. Place a large book or magazine inside the pillowcase when you print to prevent paint from coming through the material to the bottom layer. Turn the pillowcase as you work until you get back to where you began. The designs won't match perfectly at the seam where they meet, but this won't show when the pillow is inside the pillowcase.

**3**

Print the flowers in the second color, aligning the registration marks as indicated.

**4**

To set the design, follow the instructions included with the paint that you use.

**TRACE AND CUT THE
FOLLOWING STENCILS WITH
2-INCH (5 CM) BORDERS:**

1.  Leaves and stems

2.  Tulips

REPEAT

ACTUAL SIZE

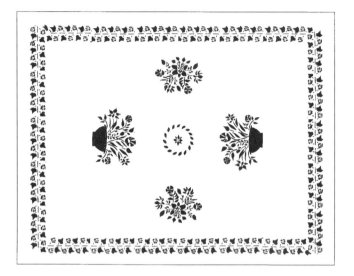

2 plain-colored, double-bed sheets (white, off-white, or very light colors are best) or fabric of appropriate size

Yardstick or tape measure

Washable fabric marker

Nine 12" x 18" (30 cm x 45 cm) stencil sheets and cutting tool

Fabric paint (3 colors)

Stencil brush

Paint tray

Quilting hoop

90" x 108" (2.3 m x 2.7 m) quilt batting

Quilting thread to match the background color

Double-fold quilt binding

A stencilled quilt is an especially stunning and satisfying project. Choose designs and colors to complement a room or imitate an old patchwork quilt. After the stencilling is completed, the designs are outlined with quilt stitching to make them stand out.

Draw your quilt to scale on a piece of graph paper and plan the placement of your design. Use washable fabric markers or chalk to mark the placement of design motifs and quilting lines on the quilt. Spread the cloth out on the floor when you mark it so that you can keep it smooth and square. You may wish to put the quilt on the floor when you stencil it, or you may find it easier to hold the cloth taut in a quilting hoop. If you use a hoop, pile newspapers under it to provide a firm surface on which to stencil.

The directions given here are for a double-bed quilt, but they can be easily adapted for any size. For the fabric, use bed sheets (with all hems and selvedges removed) or purchase wide muslin at fabric stores that specialize in quilting supplies [you will need a piece about 81" x 96" (2 m x 2.4 m)]. Many quilters prefer 100 percent cotton fabric, but a polyester-cotton blend is also appropriate. Whichever you use, launder it to remove all sizing before you begin your project. For best results, use quilting thread for your quilting stitches.

## THE STENCILLING

### 1

Cut the hems off the tops and bottoms of the sheets. Spread one sheet on the floor, and mark the exact center. Measure out from the center toward each side, and make marks at 18 and 24 inches (45 and 61 cm). Measure from the center and make marks 24 and 30

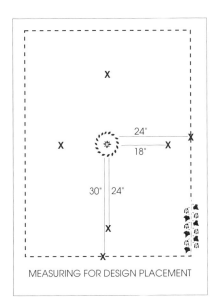

MEASURING FOR DESIGN PLACEMENT

inches (61 and 76 cm) toward the top and bottom. The outer marks indicate the position of the running border of the central panel; the inner marks locate the position of the four floral bouquets — those at the top and bottom are in containers; those on the sides are simple sprays. Extend the outer marks parallel to the edges of the fabric until they intersect at each corner.

### 2

Stencil the leaves along the running border. Position the stencil with the broken line on the guide line, and tape it down while you stencil. Follow the suggestions on pages 15-16 for printing continuous borders. When you get to a corner, keep the outside edges even. If there are blank spots you don't like when you lift the stencil, stencil in an extra leaf or flower to fill in. Continue until you reach where you started.

### 3

In the second color, print the flowers for the border, using registration marks to position the stencil.

### 4

Match the center of the circle with the center mark on the fabric, and stencil the circle with the leaf color, and then the flower in the second color.

### 5

Position the stencil with the flower-filled container so that the center bottom of the container is on the mark 6 inches (15 cm) inside the top border; the flowers should point in toward the center. Stencil another flower-filled container at the bottom of the quilt. Use the same color as used for the leaves in the border.

### 6

With the color used for the flowers in the border, stencil the large flowers in these containers. Stencil the remaining flowers in the third color. Locate these stencils with the registration marks.

### 7

Stencil the floral spray on the two remaining marks on the sides.

Position the first stencil so that the bottom leaves touch the 6-inch (15 cm) mark and all flowers but the large center flower point in to the center of the quilt. Use the same color for the leaves as you used elsewhere, and the same colors for the large and small flowers as you used for the container arrangement.

### 8

When the container is thoroughly dry, overprint the shading on it.

### 9

To set the design, follow the directions included with the paint you use.

## THE QUILTING

### 10

Put the stencilled fabric face down on the floor. Cut the batting 1 inch (2.5 cm) smaller than the

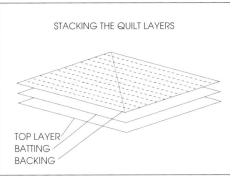

STACKING THE QUILT LAYERS

TOP LAYER
BATTING
BACKING

quilt all around, and center the batting over the quilt. Place the backing sheet on top of the batting, smooth all layers, and safety pin them together, using enough pins so you can pick up the whole thing without its falling apart. Beginning at the center of the quilt, hand baste diagonally to each corner; then baste vertically, making lines about 8 inches (20 cm) apart across the entire quilt. Finally, baste around the outside edges of the quilt, catching the batting with your stitches. In order to assure that all layers stay smooth, you may wish to leave the quilt on the floor while you are basting it.

**11**
Place the center design in a quilting hoop; pull the fabric taut and smooth on both the front and back

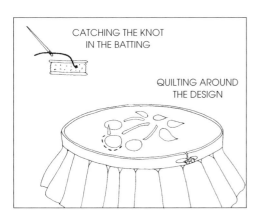

sides. To secure the end of the thread, make a small knot that you

can pull through the backing and then allow to catch in the batting where it won't show. Bring the needle to the front, coming out very near, but just outside the line of the design. Stitch with very small stitches [⅛ inch (3 mm)] all around the outside of the design, pulling the stitching tight. When you finish outlining the design, move the quilting hoop to another design.

**Note:** Instead of quilting you can simply make ties every 4 inches in both directions. Prepare the quilt top, batting, and backing in the same way as for quilting. To hold the filling in place on the edges, run a line of stitching 2 inches (5 cm) from the edge all around the quilt. For the ties, use a fairly heavy weight crochet cotton. With a threaded, large-eyed needle, come up from the back side of the quilt, leaving 3 inches (7.5 cm) of thread at the back. Return to the back side about ½ inch (1.2 cm) away from the first stitch and tie a

square knot with the ends. Clip off the thread ends to about ¾ inch (1.9 cm).

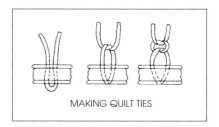

**12**
If necessary, trim the edges. Finish the edges with quilt binding. Stitch one side of the binding to the front of the quilt, right sides together, and fold the rest to the back, covering the raw edges. Machine stitch in place through all layers (or hand hem, if preferred).

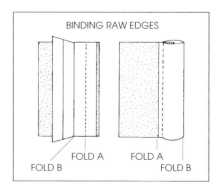

### A NOTE ON TABLECLOTHS AND BEDSPREADS

You can design and stencil a tablecloth or a bedspread in much the same way as you do a quilt. Start with a ready-made, plain-colored tablecloth, or use a wide piece of material (even a sheet). Plan your design layout on a piece of graph paper. If you wish, make a corresponding grid on the tablecloth to guide you in placing your design. Always use light pencil or chalk markings, and test a scrap of material first to be sure you will be able to launder the marks out successfully. A unique, oval or rectangular center design, with a complementary border pattern, is effective for a tablecovering. Use decorative stencils in each corner, as well.

## TRACE AND CUT THE FOLLOWING STENCILS WITH 2-INCH (5 CM) BORDERS:

1. Leaves and broken line for the border

2. Flowers for the border

3. Center circle

4. Central flower

5. Flower container, stems, and leaves

6. Large flowers in container

7. Remaining flowers in container

8. Leaves and stems for second floral bouquet (without container)

9. Large flowers for second floral bouquet

10. Remaining flowers for second floral bouquet

11. Shading for container

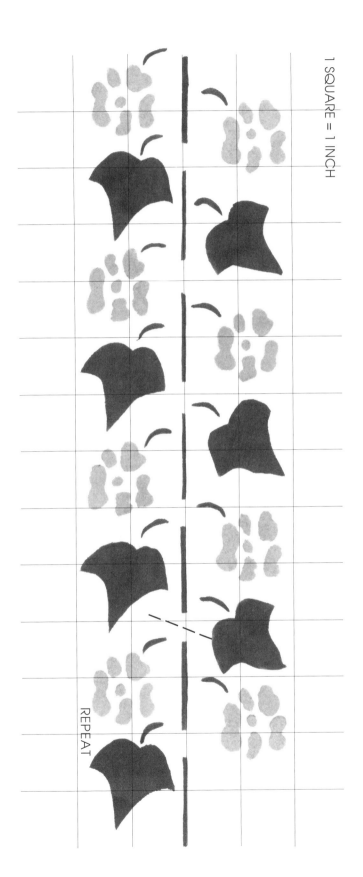

1 SQUARE = 1 INCH

REPEAT

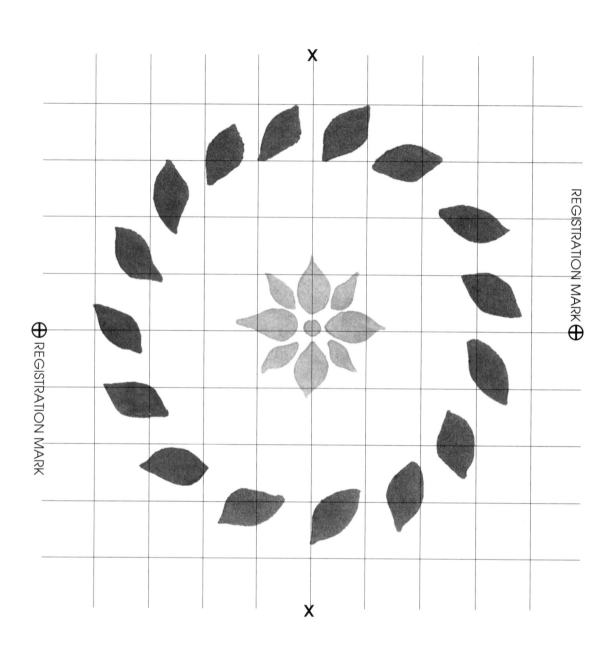

X

X

REGISTRATION MARK ⊕

⊕ REGISTRATION MARK

X                                                                              X

X

X

⊕
REGISTRATION
MARK

⊕
REGISTRATION
MARK

# STENCILLED AND QUILTED THROW PILLOWS

*(color page 94)*

Stencilled throw pillows make wonderful accents for other household furnishings. Covers are easy to make, and filling material is available in most fabric stores. For a country or old-fashioned look, off-white muslin is a good choice; for a contemporary home, a stark white fabric may be more striking. If you wish, you can quilt the pillow cover after you stencil it.

For this project, the two companion pillows have different designs, but use the same colors. To save time, print all the parts of the design that are in the same color on both pillows before proceeding to the second color. (The directions, however, give the steps for each pillow separately.) The stencilled stripes imitate velvet ribbon.

## MATERIALS

2 yards (1.8 m) of fabric

Measuring tool

Two 12" x 18" (30 cm x 45 cm) stencil sheets and cutting tool

Fabric paint (2 colors)

Stencil brush

Paint tray

Scrap paper

3-inch-wide (7.5 cm) masking tape, gummed on one half

½ yard (45 cm) of 36-inch-wide (1 m) quilt batting

Small quilting hoop

Quilting thread (to match fabric)

3¼ yards (3 m) of cording

Stuffing for two 12-inch (30 cm) pillows

## THE STENCILLING

**1**
Cut two pieces of muslin, each 14 inches (35 cm) square. Make a mark at the exact center of each.

**2**
On one square, mark a line 2 inches (5 cm) from the edge all the way around. Place masking tape along the line on *one* edge, sticky side toward the line. Lay another line of masking tape ¼ inch (6 mm) inside the first. The tape should run the whole 14-inch (35 cm) width of the pillow. Print in between the two lines. Remove the masking tape. In the same way, stencil stripes 2 inches (5 cm) from the other three edges. Remove the masking tape after stencilling each side so the stripes cross each other at the corners.

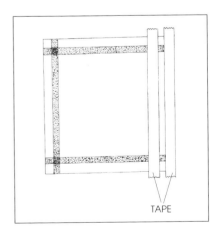

TAPE

**3**
Center the first stencil for the abstract floral pattern within the

frame created in Step 2. Tape it down so it doesn't move, and print it.

**4**

Change colors, and print the rest of the abstract floral pattern; use the registration marks to position.

**5**

On the companion pillow, print a pineapple on the diagonal in each corner. To get the designs straight, lay a ruler or yardstick across the fabric, corner to corner, and make light marks at 3 inches (7.5 cm) and 8 inches (20 cm). Mark all four corners in the same manner. Position the pineapple leaves stencil so that the center leaf touches the 8-inch (20 cm) mark. This will put the bottom of the pineapple on the 3-inch (7.5 cm) mark. Tape the stencil down, and print the leaves.

**6**

Change colors and print the center of the pineapple, using the registration marks to position the stencil correctly.

**7**

To set the design, follow the directions provided with the product you use.

**THE QUILTING**

**8**

Cut two pieces of batting each 12

inches (30 cm) square. Cut two pieces of backing, each 14 inches (35 cm) square. Place one of the stencilled pieces face down on a smooth, flat surface. On top of it and centered so 1 inch (2.5 cm) shows all around, place a square piece of batting. On top of the batting, place a square of backing. Safety pin the three layers together so you can pick them up and handle them as one piece. Run two rows of hand basting vertically and two horizontally across the pillows, about 4 inches (10 cm) apart, to stabilize the piece while you quilt.

**9**

Place one of the designs in a quilting hoop to help hold it. Follow the quilting instructions on page 128, and stitch just outside each of the designs.

**SEWING THE PILLOWCASES**

**10**

Cut two 14-inch-square (35 cm) pieces of fabric for the pillow backs. Place one of the finished quilted pieces on a flat surface, with the design facing up. Measure and lightly mark a line 1 inch (2.5 cm) from the edge all the way around the top to form a 12-inch (30 cm) square.

**11**

To make the cording for the pil-

low, cut 1-inch (2.5 cm) bias strips from the fabric, and encase cording in the bias strip. You will need about 56 inches (1.4 m) for each pillow. (Instead of using matching cording, you could use purchased piping that matches one of the colors in your design.)

Pin the cording to the quilted piece, with the cording seam *on* the guide line made in Step 10 and the raw edge of the cording facing the edge. Start and end the cording in the middle of the bottom of the pillow, and turn the ends to the raw edge of the quilted piece, butting the folds against each other. Stitch (or baste) the cording in place.

**12**

Place the pillow back over the quilted piece, right sides together. Stitch all around the pillow, just inside the cording seam. For best results, use the zipper foot on your machine so that you can get close to the cording without running over it. If you use pillow forms, leave a 10-inch (25 cm) opening at the bottom (stitching around both bottom corners), insert the pillow form, and hand-stitch the opening closed. If you use polyester fill, leave a 3- or 4-inch (7.5 or 10 cm) opening at the bottom, stuff the pillow, to the desired firmness, and then stitch the opening.

## TRACE AND CUT THE FOLLOWING STENCILS WITH 2-INCH (5 CM) BORDERS:

1. Center and outer portion of abstract floral pattern

2. Remainder of abstract floral pattern

3. Top and bottom leaves of the pineapple

4. Pineapple

REGISTRATION MARKS

1 SQUARE = 1 INCH

# STENCILLED AND QUILTED PLACEMAT AND NAPKIN SET

*(color page 91)*

Quilted placemats are fun and easy to do — and offer many design possibilities. They can be made from ready-made, plain-colored mats or from yardage. A rather simple design will fill up the space beautifully. Choose a color to complement the dining area, or create a design and use colors that coordinate with your favorite dishes. Try to do a whole set at one time, especially if you are mixing paint, so the colors on all of them will be the same. Tape both the mats and the stencil in place as you work, so you can use your hands to keep the fabric from moving.

## MATERIALS

2½ yards (2.3 m) off-white or light-colored muslin

One 12" x 18" (30 cm x 45 cm) stencil sheet and cutting tool

Measuring tools

Fabric paint (2 colors)

Stencil brush

Paint tray

Scrap paper

1 yard (1 m) of 36-inch-wide (1 m) quilt batting

Quilting thread to match fabric

A small quilting hoop

8 yards (7.3 m) of seam binding (matched or color coordinated with the stencil print)

**1**
For the placemats, cut eight 12" x 18" inch (30 cm x 45 cm) rectangles from the muslin; for the napkins, cut four 15-inch (38 cm) squares. Narrow hem the edges of the napkins.

**2**
Aligning the two sides of the stencil with the edges of the fabric, tape the stencil of the cherries into a corner of one of the napkins (the leaves should point into the center). Print the same stencil in one corner of each of the napkins and in each corner of the four placemats.

**3**
Stencil all the leaves and stems on both napkins and mats.

**4**
To set the designs, follow the instructions that are included with the paint you use.

**5**
Cut four pieces of quilt batting, 12" x 18" (30 cm x 45 cm). Place the stencilled mats face down on a firm surface. Place a piece of batting on each of them. Put a backing piece over the batting of each. Pin and baste the three pieces together.

**6**
Place one of the designs in a quilting hoop. So you won't have a knot on the back of the placemat, bring a needle and knotted thread up to the front from the batting layer, (see page 128). Take very small stitches (⅛ inch (3 mm)

long) to outline the entire design. When the thread gets short, tie it on the inside in the batting, and start the new thread so the line of stitching appears to be unbroken.

## 7

Quilt another cherry outline at the center, both to provide a decorative quilted accent and to hold the mat together. Mark the exact cen-

ter of the placemat, and center the design on the mark. Trace both parts of the cherry pattern very lightly in pencil or chalk onto the placemat. Quilt around the lines.

## 8

Finish the placemat by sewing seam binding around the edges. (See page 128.)

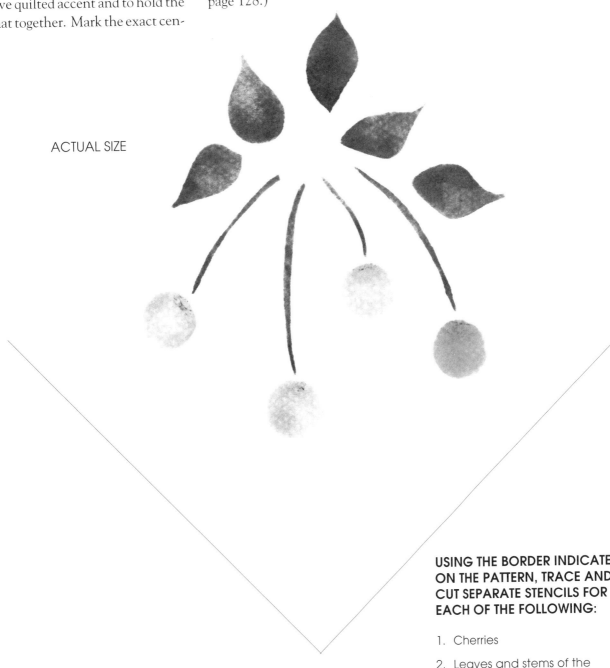

ACTUAL SIZE

**USING THE BORDER INDICATED ON THE PATTERN, TRACE AND CUT SEPARATE STENCILS FOR EACH OF THE FOLLOWING:**

1. Cherries

2. Leaves and stems of the cherries

# STENCILLED AND QUILTED HOT PADS

*(color page 91)*

T he four hot pads in this set have the same leaf patterns, but each has a different blossom.

## MATERIALS

½ yard (45 cm) of plain-colored, 36- or 45-inch (90 or 115 cm) wide, cotton fabric and thread to match (for four hot pads)

Three 9" x 12" (23 cm x 30 cm) stencil sheets and cutting tool

Fabric paint (3 colors)

Stencil brush

Paint tray

Scrap paper

¼ yard (23 cm) of 36-inch-wide (90 cm) quilt batting (100 percent cotton is preferable for heat resistance)

Quilting hoop

Contrasting single-fold bias tape (matched to one of the paint colors)

Compass and pencil

**1**
Cut the fabric into 9-inch (23 cm) squares; you will need two squares per hot pad. Cut the batting into squares ¼ inch (6 mm) smaller all around than the cloth squares; use one square per hot pad.

**2**
Make a mark at the center of each hot pad, 2 inches (5 cm) up from the bottom. Place the registration mark indicated on the leaf stencil on this mark. Stencil the leaves and stems on each of the hot pads.

**3**
Stencil the flowers, printing two of each color.

**4**
To set the design, follow the directions included with your paint.

**5**
To quilt the pad, place the stencilled square face down on a table. On top of it, place the batting, and then an unstencilled fabric square

for backing. Pin the pieces in place. Place the pad in a quilting hoop. So you won't have a knot on the back of the hot pad, bring a needle and knotted thread up to the front from the batting layer. Taking small stitches [⅛ inch (3 mm)], stitch just outside the flower and leaves. Stitch around the design through all the layers of material; pull the stitches tight as you work. When you need to tie off the thread, fold the backing aside, so you can tie off in the batting layer and hide the end. Quilt all four hot pads.

**6**
With a compass, mark a very light circle around the outside of each flower, and quilt around the circles.

**7**
Finish the edges by covering them with bias tape (see page 128). Make hanging loops from short lengths of tape.

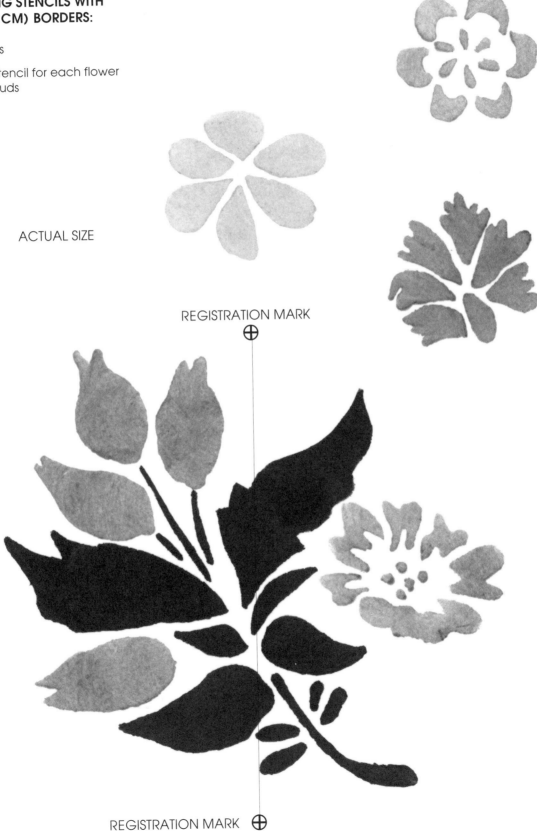

**TRACE AND CUT THE
FOLLOWING STENCILS WITH
2-INCH (5 CM) BORDERS:**

1.  Leaves

2-5. One stencil for each flower
     and buds

ACTUAL SIZE

REGISTRATION MARK
⊕

REGISTRATION MARK ⊕

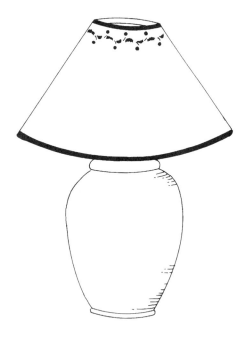

The stencilled "velvet" ribbon around the top and bottom of the lamp shade is made by printing between two pieces of masking tape over the fabric covering the wire frame that supports the shade.

## MATERIALS

A white or off-white lamp shade

3-inch-wide (7.5 cm) masking tape, gummed on one half

1-inch-wide (2.5 cm) masking tape

One 9" x 12" (23 cm x 30 cm) stencil sheet and cutting tool

Stencil paints (2 colors)

Stencil brush

Paint tray

Paint thinner

Scrap paper

**1**

Beginning at the top of the back seam, tuck the masking tape as close to the fabric covering the frame as possible — even behind it, if you can. Place the gummed edge toward the top and the un-gummed side toward the bottom. Place a line of 1-inch (2.5 cm) masking tape along the top of the shade, so you don't get paint on the back. Follow this same procedure at the bottom of the shade. Stencil between the lines of tape, at both top and bottom, using a very dry brush. As you work, support the shade from the back with your free hand.

**2**

Make light pencil marks ½ inch (1.2 cm) down from the bottom of the stencilled "ribbon" all around the top of the shade. Tape the leaves-and-branch stencil to the lamp shade, starting at the back seam; the top of the design (*not* the

top of the stencil) should be against the guide line. Follow the instructions on pages 15-16 for printing continuous borders, and stencil the design around the top.

**3**

Tape the berry stencil over the printed border, using the registration marks for positioning. Stencil the berries in the second color.

**TRACE AND CUT THE FOLLOWING STENCILS WITH 2-INCH (5 CM) BORDERS:**

1. Leaves and branches

2. Berries (you may be able to cut the berries with a hole punch)

REPEAT

ACTUAL SIZE

A plain white lamp base, stencilled with a simple floral motif, provides an elegant decorative accent with little effort or cost.

Rounded, slippery surfaces can present special challenges. This is a good project for which to use adhesive spray to hold the stencil in place; alternatively, you can cut your stencil from adhesive paper.

## MATERIALS

A plain lamp base

0-grade steel wool

One 12" x 18" (30 cm x 45 cm) stencil sheet and cutting tool

Adhesive stencil spray

Stencil paint (2 colors)

Stencil brush

Paint tray

Scrap paper

Paint thinner and clean cloths

**1**

If your lamp base is ceramic, paint will not adhere well to the glazed surface; you must therefore etch the surface of the lamp base by rubbing it with the fine steel wool to remove the sheen. Go over the entire surface, using the same hand motion (circular or side to side) as you rub, to create as even a texture as possible. Rub only enough to provide a surface that will accept paint.

**2**

Tape the stencil for the leaves and stem of the iris onto the lamp base centered on the side opposite the lamp cord. Stencil the image. This print will look best if very lightly applied. Allow the paint to dry.

**3**

Tape the iris blossom stencil in place and print it.

**TRACE AND CUT THE
FOLLOWING STENCILS WITH
2-INCH (5 CM) BORDERS:**

1.  Stem and leaves

2.  Iris blossom

REGISTRATION MARK

REGISTRATION MARK

ACTUAL SIZE

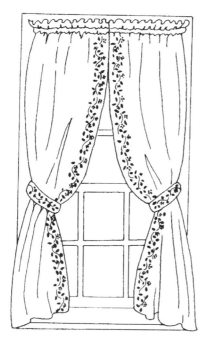

When you want just a bit of color on your curtains, but not a completely patterned fabric, stencilling is the ideal solution, on either ready-made, plain-colored curtains or those you sew. You can place your design neatly along the edges where you want it and create your own unique fabric border. You can stencil only lengthwise down the curtain, make a running border along both edges *and* bottom, and/or stencil the tiebacks.

## MATERIALS

Several yards of plain-colored fabric and matching thread

One 12" x 18" (30 cm x 45 cm) stencil sheet and cutting tool

Fabric paint (2 colors)

Stencil brush

Paint tray

Scrap paper

**1**

To sew the curtains, measure your window from the top of the top casing to the sill, and cut a piece of material 8 inches (20 cm) longer than this measurement. The total width of the pair of curtains should be about twice the width of the window. Cut off the selvedges, and turn 1-inch (2.5 cm) hems along the long edges.

**2**

Fold down the top of the material 3½ inches (9 cm), wrong sides together; press. Stitch 1 inch (2.5 cm) from the fold all along the top. Turn the raw edge under about ⅜ inch (1 cm). Topstitch the hem in place, 2 inches (5 cm) down from the first stitching, close to the fold. The opening between the two lines of stitching is the casing for the curtain rod. Prepare the second curtain the same way.

**3**

Make the tiebacks by cutting a piece of material 6 inches (15 cm) wide and as long as needed [usually about 15 inches (38 cm)]. Fold it in half lengthwise, right sides together, and stitch. Turn the tieback right side out, and flatten the piece so that the seam is centered on the back; press. Fold the raw edges of the ends to the inside and stitch them in place.

**4**

Hang the curtains on a rod in your window. Mark the bottom hem length, and pin the hem in place. Use the tiebacks to pull the curtains back before you stitch the hem to be sure the curtains are the right length.

**5**

With the leaves and vine stencil, print a continuous border down the inside edges of the curtains and along the tiebacks. Place the curtain flat on a table and tape the stencils in place when you work. Place the edge of the stencil along the edge of the cloth. Follow the suggestions on pages 15-16 for printing continuous borders. If you wish, you can continue the border along the bottom, as well.

**6**

Print the flowers, using the registration marks to locate the design.

**7**

To set the design, follow the directions that are included with the paint you use.

REPEAT

REGISTRATION MARK

REGISTRATION MARK

ACTUAL SIZE

**TRACE AND CUT THE FOLLOWING STENCILS, WITH 1½-INCH (4 CM) BORDERS:**

1. Leaves and vine

2. Flowers

These customized drapes feature a stencilled border along the vertical edges and large bouquets of flowers evenly spaced between the pleats.

## MATERIALS

Plain drapery and lining fabric, and thread to match

Four 12" x 18" (30 cm x 45 cm) stencil sheets and cutting tool

Tape measure

Fabric paint (3 colors)

Stencil brush

Paint tray

Scrap paper

**1**

Stitch together as many panels as necessary to get the correct width for your drapes. Iron the seams flat. Spread the piece out on the floor. (Protect the floor with newspapers, in case paint seeps through.) Plan the placement of the pleats, and then find and mark the center of the sections of the drapes that will not be pleated. With chalk or water-soluble fabric marking pen, draw lines from these centers to the hem, exactly parallel to the edges of the drapes; these are the guide lines for the floral bouquets. Plan the spacing of these bouquets so that the top one begins 12 inches (30 cm) from the top edge, and the bottom one ends 9 inches (23 cm) above the bottom edge. Space the other bouquets evenly between these, about 10 inches (25 cm) apart.

**2**

Print the leaves on both drapes first.

**3**

With the second color, print the small flowers on both drapes.

**4**

With the same color as used in Step 3, print the centers of the border flowers. Place the edge of the stencil against the raw edge of the fabric, so that the design is printed 2 inches (5 cm) from the edge. Begin the continuous border at the top so that a whole flower will appear just below the top edge after you have formed the heading. Print to the hemline, again planning the prints so that a whole flower completes the design just above the hem.

**5**

With the third color, print the remaining flowers in the bouquet, and the petals of the border flowers.

**6**

To set the design, follow the instructions that are provided with the paint you use. If you are considering dry cleaning your drapes, check to be sure the manufacturer guarantees the colors will hold up being treated with those chemicals.

**7**

Complete the construction of the drapes.

REPEAT

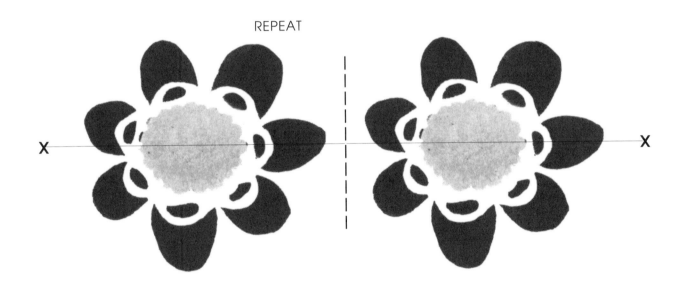

ACTUAL SIZE

**TRACE AND CUT THE FOLLOWING STENCILS WITH 2-INCH (5 CM) BORDERS:**

1. Leaves and stems of floral bouquets

2. Small flowers and buds for floral bouquets

3. Large flowers for floral bouquets

4. Border flower centers

5. Border flower petals

X                                                                          X

# 7 STENCILLING ON PAPER

Many papers are just absorbent enough to take a beautiful stencil print, and stencilled papers offer a wealth of ideas for gift giving—from the gift itself (stencilled stationery, for example)—to the card you tuck into the gift box and the paper with which you wrap it.

Any weight paper is suitable, but different kinds of paper, as well as various paint applicators, produce different textural effects. You can use the same paints as you do for wall, furniture, or fabric stencilling; japan paints work especially well for paper projects, because they dry quickly and give a flat finish. If you are working with children, poster paint (either premixed or powdered) makes for easy clean up; it is also readily applied with a sponge. Children may also enjoy using marking pens or even ordinary crayons.

The pattern for stationery should, of course, be small and relatively simple. The design may be centered, placed in one corner, or stencilled as a border all around the page. Young children like stationery with their names stencilled at the top (for stencil alphabet, see page 157). Flowers, boats, ducks, mice, and ladybugs all make nice motifs for stationery.

When designing gift wrap, anything goes. Wrapping paper can be made out of any paper that doesn't tear too easily. White or off-white freezer paper is a good choice, or use plain-colored rolls of gift wrap and personalize them with your own design. Make it easy for yourself, and choose a stencil that is not too complicated.

To stencil gift wrap, spread out the paper, right side up. Freezer paper sometimes has one side that is a little waxy, and since paint won't easily adhere to the shiny side, print on the other side. Measure for placement of the design. A very regular, all-over design may be placed on a diagonal, parallel, or perpendicular to the long sides. In any case, rule in a large-squared grid very lightly in pencil. Such a grid makes it easy to position your designs. Nothing however, says that the design must be symmetrical. A free-flowing, irregularly placed pattern can be interesting and imaginative, as long as the whole paper is covered with figures. You can also stencil designs on plain paper *after* you wrap the package. This allows you to feature the stencils where they are most effective for a very customized look (see page 96).

A striking paper can be made by reverse stencilling: place leaves or other objects on the paper to block the color, and spray lightly with spray paint. Or, save cutouts from your stencils and use them to block spray. Experiment with using both "positive" and "negative" images on your paper. Keep the spray can far enough from the paper so that the force of the air coming from the nozzle doesn't move the stencil cut-outs and blur the design.

# GIFT WRAP

*(color page 96)*

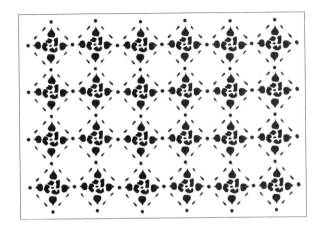

**1**

Cut a piece of paper 36 inches (1 m) long. Place a light pencil mark every 2 inches (5 cm) both lengthwise and crosswise.

**2**

Position the center of the flower on a 2-inch (5 cm) mark and each circle on the marks above, below, and beside it. Print this stencil. When you position the next stencil, do not paint over the already printed parts. Print the leaves in the second color.

**3**

Print the remaining stencil in the third color.

## MATERIALS

1 roll of shelf paper, freezer paper, or plain gift wrap

Three 9" x 12" (23 cm x 30 cm) stencil sheets and cutting tool

Measuring tool

Stencil paints (3 colors)

Stencil brush

Paint tray

Scrap paper

Paint thinner

ACTUAL SIZE

REGISTRATION MARKS

**TRACE AND CUT THE FOLLOWING STENCILS, WITH 2-INCH (5 CM) BORDERS:**

1. Flower and circles

2. Leaves

3. Outer broken edge

Two blossom shapes are included with this pattern. Each is used in the same position in relation to the stem. Use as many colors as you wish to create a set of stationery.

## MATERIALS

Plain stationery of good-quality paper, and envelopes to match

One 9" x 12" (23 cm x 30 cm) stencil sheet and cutting tool

Metal ruler

Stencil paint (3 colors)

Stencil brush

Paint tray

Paint thinner and clean cloths

Scrap paper

**1**

When you cut the stencils, place the edges of the stencil material on the right-angle guide line shown on page 153. You can then align the stencil edges with the edges of the stationery when you print the design.

**2**

Print the leaves and bars in one color.

**3**

The two flower designs are interchangeable. Print each design in several different colors if you wish.

**TRACE AND CUT THE
FOLLOWING STENCILS, WITH
2-INCH (5 CM) BORDERS:**

1.  Stems and leaves

2-3. Flowers

4.  2-inch (5 cm) bar

ACTUAL SIZE

The little snow-covered town looks especially handsome done on dark-colored paper, such as blue, green, or maroon. Look for cards with matching envelopes in art-supply stores, or create your own colored envelopes. This project requires three stencils. The snow for the mountains and town is printed first, the houses are overprinted on the snow, and, finally, the windows and doors are overprinted on the houses. (When overprinting, always be sure that the undercoat is thoroughly dry before proceeding.) For an interesting, soft texture, try stencilling the snow with a sponge instead of a brush. The opacity of japan paints or oil-based silk-screen printing inks works well for this project.

The iris pattern stencil can be found on page 143 (Lamp Base). Many other patterns, or parts of patterns, in the book would be equally fine for this purpose (see page 96).

## MATERIALS

20 blank cards (not white)

One 12" x 18" (30 cm x 45 cm) stencil sheet and cutting tool

Stencil paint (white, a color for the houses, and black)

Stencil brush and/or sponges cut into 1-inch (2.5 cm) squares

Paint tray

Paint thinner and clean cloths

Scrap paper

**1**
Center the stencil with the snow-covered portions of the design on the front of each card and print. Lay the cards out while they dry completely.

**2**
Stencil the houses.

**3**
Stencil the black windows and doors, using a very dry brush.

**TRACE AND CUT THE
FOLLOWING STENCILS, WITH
2-INCH (5 CM) BORDERS:**

1.  Snow-covered objects
    (appear as gray on stencil
    pattern)

2.  Houses

3.  Windows, doors, and chimneys

REGISTRATION MARK

REGISTRATION MARK

ACTUAL SIZE

A B C D E
F G H I J
K L M N O
P Q R S T
U V W X Y Z
1 2 3 4 5
6 7 8 9 0

# INDEX